Bailegangaire

Methuen

First published in 1986 by The Gallery Press, Dublin, Ireland
Reprinted in a revised version in 1988 by Methuen London Ltd ·
Reprinted, with revisions, in *Tom Murphy Plays: 2* in 1993
by Methuen Drama

This edition published in 2001 by
Methuen Publishing Ltd
215 Vauxhall Bridge Road
London SW1V 1EJ

www.methuen.co.uk

Copyright © 1986, 1988, 1993 by Tom Murphy

Tom Murphy has asserted his rights under the Copyright, Designs
and Patents Act, 1988, to be identified as the author of this work

Methuen Publishing Ltd reg. number 3543167

ISBN 0 413 77121 0

A CIP catalogue record for this book is available at the British Library

Transferred to digital printing 2004

Caution

The National Theatre
The Abbey and Peacock Theatres

Bailegangaire

by Tom Murphy

Methuen Drama

This edition of **Bailegangaire** has been re-published
to coincide with the Abbey and Peacock Theatre's major season
of plays by Tom Murphy held in October 2001.

The National Theatre gratefully acknowledges the financial
support from the Arts Council/An Chomhairle Ealaíon

Bailegangaire

by Tom Murphy

Bailegangaire by Tom Murphy opened at the Peacock Theatre on 5 October, 2001.

The play is set in 1984 in the kitchen of a thatched house.

Cast

Mommo	Pauline Flanagan
Mary	Jane Brennan
Dolly	Derbhle Crotty
Director	Tom Murphy
Set Designer	Bláithín Sheerin
Costume Designer	Joan O'Clery
Lighting Designer	Paul Keogan
Sound	Dave Nolan
Assistant Director	Tom Conway
Stage Director	Angie White
Assistant Stage Manager	Nicola Teehan
Festival Producer	Una Carmody
Voice Coach	Andrea Ainsworth
Set	Abbey Theatre Workshop
Costumes	Abbey Theatre Wardrobe Department

Tom Murphy

Plays include:

On the Outside *(w. Noel O'Donoghue)*
A Whistle in the Dark
The Orphans
A Crucial Week in the Life of a Grocer's Assistant
Famine
The Morning After Optimism
The White House
On the Inside
The Sanctuary Lamp
The J. Arthur Maginnis Story
Epitaph Under Ether *(a compilation from the works of J.M.Synge)*
The Blue Macushla
The Informer *(from the novel by Liam O'Flaherty)*
Conversations on a Homecoming
The Gigli Concert
Bailegangaire
A Thief of a Christmas
Too Late for Logic
The Patriot Game
Cupa Coffee
She Stoops to Folly *(from The Vicar of Wakefield)*
The Wake
The House

And a novel, **The Seduction of Morality**

He has received numerous awards and nominations.
Awards include: Irish Academy of Letters Award, Harveys Irish Theatre Award (twice), Sunday Tribune Arts Award, Independent Newspapers Theatre Award, Sunday Independent/Irish Life Award, Drama-Logue Critics Award, Irish Times/ESB Lifetime Award, Irish Times/ESB Theatre Award (Best Play) and Honorary Degrees from University of Dublin (Trinity College) and NUI (Galway). He was born in Tuam, County Galway. He lives in Dublin.

Bláithín Sheerin *Designer*

Bláithín trained in sculpture and performance art at NCAD and in theatre design at Motley @ Riverside Studios, London. Previous work at the Abbey and Peacock Theatres includes **Eden, Made in China, As the Beast Sleeps** and **You Can't Take it with You.** Other designs include **The Comedy of Errors**, RSC, **Our Father,** Almeida Theatre, **The Importance of Being Earnest**, West Yorkshire Playhouse, **Juno and the Paycock,** Lyric Theatre, **The Beckett Festival** (composite set design), Gate Theatre, John Jay Theatre, New York. She has designed for Druid, Groundwork, Charabanc, Red Kettle, TEAM, The Ark, Second Age and Prime Cut theatre companies. Her designs for Rough Magic Theatre Company include **Midden, The Whisperers, The School for Scandal, Northern Star, Pentecost, The Way of the World, The Dogs, Digging for Fire** and **Love and a Bottle**.

Joan O'Clery *Costume Designer*

Joan's work at the Abbey and Peacock Theatres includes **Blackwater Angel, The House, The Tempest, The Wake** which toured to the Edinburgh Festival, **The Freedom of the City,** which toured to the Lincoln Center, New York and **The Colleen Bawn** which toured to the Royal National Theatre, London, **Kevin's Bed, Give Me Your Answer, Do!, A Woman of No Importance, Macbeth, The Only True History of Lizzie Finn, Philadelphia, Here I Come!, Observe the Sons of Ulster Marching Towards the Somme, Sive, The Last Apache Reunion, Rumpelstiltskin, The Third Law of Motion, Something's in the Way** and **Toupees and Snaredrums,** a CoisCéim/Abbey Theatre co-production. Joan designed the costumes for the Gate Theatre's production of **Oleanna** and was the winner of the 1997 Irish Times/ESB Costume Designer of the Year Award for her work on the Gate Theatre's **Pinter Festival**. Last year she designed the costumes for **Peer Gynt** at the Royal National Theatre, London. She also designed **Sive** by John B. Keane, Palace Theatre, Watford and Tricycle, **Licking the Marmalade Spoon,** Project Arts Centre and **Judith** at project @ the mint.

Paul Keogan *Lighting Designer*

Born in Dublin Paul studied Drama at the Samuel Beckett Centre, Trinity College Dublin and at Glasgow University. Paul was Production Manager for Project Arts Centre from 1994 to 1996. His designs for the Abbey and Peacock Theatres include **Melonfarmer, The Electrocution of Children, Amazing Grace, Living Quarters, Making History, The Map Maker's Sorrow, Cúirt an Mheán Oíche, Treehouses, Mrs Warren's Profession, Eden, The Tempest** and **Tartuffe.** Other work includes **Down onto Blue, Danti Dan,** Rough Magic Theatre Company, **The Silver Tassie,** Almeida Theatre, **The Gay Detective,** Project Arts Centre, **Electroshock, Quartet** and **Quay West,** Bedrock Productions, **La Bohème, L'Elisir d'Amore, The Marriage of Figaro, Madama Butterfly, Lady Macbeth of Mtsensk** and **The Silver Tassie,** Opera Ireland, **The Lighthouse,** Opera Theatre Company, **The Makropulos Case,** Opera Zuid, Netherlands, **Ballads, Seasons** and **Straight with Curves,** CoisCéim, **Sweat, Beautiful Tomorrow** and **Without Hope or Fear,** Mandance, **Territorial Claims, Chimera,** Daghdha, **SAMO,** Block & Steel, **Macalla, Intimate Gold,** Irish Modern Dance Theatre, **Angel-Babel,** Operating Theatre, **The Whiteheaded Boy,** Barabbas, **Much Ado about Nothing,** Bickerstaffe, **The Spirit of Annie Ross,** Druid Theatre Company, **The Wishing Well,** a large scale outdoor projection piece for Kilkenny Arts Festival 1999, and most recently, **Too Late for Logic** by Tom Murphy, Edinburgh International Festival.

The Abbey Theatre would like to thank:

Sponsors
Aer Lingus
Anglo Irish Bank
Calouste Gubenkian Foundation
Ferndale Films
Dr. A. J. F. O'Reilly
Oman Moving & Storage
RTE
Smurfit Ireland Ltd
Viacom Outdoor
The Irish Times

Benefactors
Aer Rianta
AIB Group
An Post
Behaviour and Attitudes
eircom
Electricity Supply Board
Independent News and Media PLC
Irish Life & Permanent plc
IIB Bank
Merc Partners
John & Viola O'Connor
Pfizer International Bank Europe
Scottish Provident Ireland
SDS
SIPTU
Unilever Ireland plc
VHI

Patrons
J. G. Corry
Brian Friel
Guinness Ireland Group
Irish Actors Equity
Gerard Kelly & Co
McCullough-Mulvin Architects
Mercer Ltd
Smurfit Corrugated Cases
Sumitomo Finance (Dublin)
Total Print and Design
Francis Wintle

**Sponsors of the
National Theatre Archive**
Jane & James O'Donoghue
Sarah & Michael O'Reilly
Rachel & Victor Treacy

Friends of the Abbey
Patricia Barnett
Mr. Ron Bolger
Ms. Patricia Brown
Ms. Ann Byrne
Mr. Joseph Byrne
Ms. Zita Byrne
Lilian & Robert Chambers
Ms. Orla Cleary
Claire Cronin
Ms. Dolores Deacon
Ms. Patricia Devlin
Karen Doull
Paul & Florence Flynn
Ms. Christina Goldrick
Mrs. Rosaleen Hardiman
Sean & Mary Holahan
Mrs. Madeleine Humphreys
Ms. Eileen Jackson
Ms. Kate Kavanagh
Mr. Francis Keenan
Mr. Peter Keenan
Vivienne & Kieran Kelly
Joan & Michael Keogh
Donal & Máire Lowry
Mr. Fechin Maher
Una M. Moran
McCann FitzGerald Solicitors
Ellie McCullough
Mr. Joseph McCullough
Marcella & Aidan McDonnell
Liam MacNamara
Dr. Chris Morash
Mr. Frank Murray
Mr. Vincent O'Doherty
Ms. Mary O'Driscoll
Mr. Dermot & Ita O'Sullivan
Mr. Andrew Parkes
Mr. Terry Patmore
Dr. Colette Pegum
Mr. Michael P. Quinn
Mr. Noel Ryan
Breda & Brendan Shortall
Fr. Frank Stafford

Personnel

Board
James Hickey
(Chairman)
Bernard Farrell
John Fanning
Eithne Healy
Jennifer Johnston
John McColgan
Pauline Morrison
Niall O'Brien
Deirdre Purcell

Artistic Director
Ben Barnes

Managing Director
Richard Wakely

General Manager
Martin Fahy

Director's Office
Ciara Flynn
(P.A. to Artistic Director)
Grainne Howe
(P.A. Secretary)

Associate Directors
Garry Hynes
Lazlo Marton
Paul Mercier
Katie Mitchell
Conall Morrison
Lynne Parker
Deborah Warner

Casting Director
Marie Kelly

Abbey Players
Clive Geraghty
Des Cave

Staff Director
David Parnell

Voice
Andrea Ainsworth

Writer-In-Association
sponsored by
Anglo Irish Bank
Jim Nolan

Archive
Mairead Delaney (Archivist)

Honorary Associate Directors
Vincent Dowling
Tomas MacAnna

Education
Sharon Murphy (Head of
Outreach/Education)
Sarah Jordan
(Administrator)
Jean O'Dwyer
(Projects Officer)
Joanna Parkes
(Projects Officer)

Finance
Margaret Bradley
(Financial Controller)
Margaret Flynn
(Accounts)
Pat O'Connell
(Payroll)

Front of House
House Management
Pauline Morrison
(House Manager)
John Baynes
(Deputy House Manager)

Ushers
Jim O'Keeffe
(Chief Usher)
Daniel Byrne
Kevin Clarke
Ruth Colgen
Con Doyle
Ivan Kavanagh
Simon Lawlor
Seamus Mallin
Fred Murray

Box Office
Adam Lawlor
(Box Office Manager)
Des Byrne
(Box Office Assistant)
Clare Downey
(Chief Cashier)

Box Office Clerks
Catherine Casey
Anne Marie Doyle
Edel Hanly
Lorraine Hanna
Maureen Robertson
David Windrim

Cleaning
Joe McNamara
(Supervisor)

Reception
Niamh Douglas
(Senior Receptionist)
Sandra Williams
(Receptionist)

Stage Door
Patrick Gannon
Patrick Whelan

Literary
Judy Friel
(Literary Manager)
Jocelyn Clarke
(Commissioning Manager)
Orla Flanagan
(Literary Officer)

Press and Marketing
PR Representation
Kate Bowe PR
Katherine Brownridge
(Marketing Manager)
Tina Connell
(Promotions Officer)
Lucy McKeever (Press &
Programmes Officer)

Technical
Tony Wakefield
(Technical Director)
Tommy Nolan
(Production Manager)
Peter Rose
(Construction Manager)
Vanessa Fitz-Simon (Asst.
Production Manager)

Carpenters
Mark Joseph Darley
(Master Carpenter)
John Kavanagh
(Deputy)
Al Carroll
Brian Comiskey
Kenneth Crowe
(Assistant)

Scenic Artists
Vincent Bell
Angie Benner
Jennifer Moonan

Design
Emma Cullen
(Design Assistant)

Electricians
Eddie Breslin
Mick Doyle
(Chief Electrician)
Barry Fairbrother
Joe Glasgow
Barry Madden
Kevin McFadden
(Acting Deputy)

Information Technology
Dave O'Brien
(Manager)

Maintenance
Brian Fennell (Maintenance
Engineer)
Tony Delaney
(Assistant)

Props
Stephen Molloy
(Property Master)

Stage Managers
John Andrews
Gerry Doyle

Stage Hands
Aaron Clear
Mick Doyle (Flymaster)
Pat Dillon
Paul Kelly

Stage Directors
Finola Eustace
(Head of Department)
John Stapleton
Audrey Hession
Angie White

Assistant Stage Managers
Catriona Behan
Stephen Dempsey
Maree Kearns
John Sherrard
Nicola Teehan

Sound
Dave Nolan
(Chief Sound Technician)
Cormac Carroll
Nuala Golden

Wardrobe
Joan O'Clery (Acting
Wardrobe Supervisor)
Fiona Talbot
(Acting Deputy)
Angela Hanna
Vicky Miller
Frances Kelly
(Wigs & Hairdressing)
Patsy Giles
(Make-Up)

Bailegangaire

*The Story of Bailegangaire
and how it came by its appellation*

Bailegangaire was first performed by the Druid Theatre Company, Galway, on 5 December 1985 with the following cast:

Mommo   Siobhán McKenna
Mary   Marie Mullen
Dolly   Mary McEvoy

Directed by Garry Hynes
Designed by Frank Conroy
Lighting by Roger Frith

Time and place: 1984, the kitchen of a thatched house. The set should be stylized.

Note: 'Notturno' in E Flat by Schubert introduces and closes the play. Mary's poem, which she misquotes, in Act One is 'Silences' by Thomas Hardy.

Act One

Dusk is setting in on a room, a country kitchen. There are some modern conveniences: a cooker, a radio, electric light – a single pendant. Framed photographs on the walls, brown photographs of uncles, one of a christening party. There is a double bed. It is the warmest room in the house (probably the central room of the traditional three-roomed thatched house). An old woman in the bed, **Mommo**, *is eating and drinking something out of a mug, occasionally rejecting pieces of food, spitting them on the floor. She is a good mimic. She interrupts her meal –*

Mommo Shkoh cake –! Shkoth!

Driving imagined hens from the house.

Dirty aul' things about the place . . . And for all they lay!

She is senile.

Mary, *her granddaughter, is doing something. She wears a wrap-around apron draped tightly about her spinster frame; bare knees over half wellington boots; hair tight, perhaps in a bun. She is forty-one. A 'private' person, an intelligent, sensitive woman, a trier, but one who is near breaking point. It is lovely when she laughs.* **Mommo** *has again interrupted her meal, this time to talk to imagined children at the foot of the bed.*

Let ye be settling now, my fondlings, and I'll be giving ye a nice story again tonight when I finish this. For isn't it a good one? An' ye'll be goin' to sleep.

The kettle is boiling. **Mary** *makes tea, lays the table. She produces the anomaly of a silver teapot . . .* **Mommo** *is now watching* **Mary** *and* **Mary**'*s movements suspiciously.*

. . . An' no one will stop me! Tellin' my nice story . . . (*Reverts to herself.*) Yis, how the place called Bochtán – and its *graund* (*grand*) inhabitants – came by its new appellation, Bailegangaire, the place without laughter. Now! . Jolter-headed gobshites . . . (*Grandly.*) Ooh! and

to be sure, and I often heard it said, it had one time its
portion of jollification and mirth. But, I'm thinkin', the
breed they wor (*were*) 'twas venom, and the dent of it, was
ever the more customary manifestation. The land there so
poor – Ahona-ho gus hah-haa, land! – when 'twasn't bog
'twas stone, and as for the weather? 'twas credited with
bein' seven times worse than elsewhere in the kingdom.
And so hard they had it, to keep life itself in them,
whenever Bochtán was mentioned the old people in their
wisdom would add in precaution, go bhfóire Dia orainn,
may God protect us. What time is it?

Mary Seven.

Mary *is taking off her apron.*

Mommo Yis! Shkoth! – an' lock them in. Och-haw, but
I'll out-do the fox, I'll take the head of the everyone of
them tomorrow. Ooh! and to be sure –

Mary (*quietly*) Mommo?

Mommo And I often heard it said –

Mary Mommo? (*She has removed her apron and in her new
image is smiling bravely against an increasing sense of loneliness
and demoralisation.*) I have a surprise for you.

Mommo Pardon?

Mary Look! (*She holds up an iced cake.*) We never knew
your birthday but today is mine and I thought we might
share the same birthday together in future. (*She has lit a
candle.*)

Mommo (*eyes fixed on the candle*) The cursèd paraffin.

Mary Though someone said once – I may be wrong –
yours was the first of May, a May child.

Mommo The cursèd paraffin.

Mary And you can stay up for a while – if you wish.

Mommo Birthday?

Mary   Yes! We'll have a party, the two of us.

Mommo   What's birthdays to do with us?

Mary   By candlelight.

Mommo   What's your business here?

Mary (*indicating the table*)   Isn't that nice?

Mommo   Do I know you?

Mary   Mary. (*She bows her head, momentarily deflated, then smiles invitingly at* **Mommo** *again.*) Hmm?

Mommo (*and there is defiance, hatred in the sound*)   Heh heh heh heh.

Mary   Mary.

Mary *picks up a book en route to switch on the radio and sits at the table to have her tea. We get the end of the news in Irish on the radio, then Tommy O'Brien's programme of light classics,* Your Choice and Mine. *The candlelight, the table neatly laid, the silver teapot, the simple line of Mary's dress becomes her, the book beside her, sipping tea, the grave intelligent face, a picture of strange elegance.* **Mommo** *has been continuing.*

Mommo   Ooh! and to be sure and so as not to be putting any over-enlargement on my narrative, the creatures left in it now can still *smile*, on occasion. And to be sure, the childre, as is the wont of all childre in God's kingdom on earth, are as clever at the laughing as they are at the crying, until they arrive at the age of reason. That is well, my dears. Now to tell my story. Here! You! Miss! Take this. Did you manage to poison me! Ha-haa – No – ho-ho!

Mary (*takes a cup of tea to* **Mommo** *and places it on the chair beside the bed, takes the mug*)   I'll get you a nice slice of cake to go with the tea.

Mommo   Pardon?

Mary   And isn't that nice music?

Mommo   Cake?

Mary   Every Sunday night.

Mommo   Music?

Mary   Yes. Listen.

Mommo   . . . An' no one will stop me tellin' it!

Mary, *suspended in the action of about to cut the cake, now sits at the table, lights a cigarette, face impassive, exhaling smoke.*

Mommo (*settles herself in the bed for her story*)   Now . . . It was a bad year for the crops, a good one for mushrooms and the contrary and adverse connection between these two is always the case. So you can be sure the people were putting their store in the poultry and the bonavs (*bonhams*) and the creamery produce for the great maragadh mór (*big market*) that is held every year on the last Saturday before Christmas in Bailethuama (the town of Tuam) in the other county. And some sold well and some sold middlin', and one couple was in it – strangers, ye understand – sold not at all. And at day's business concluded there was celebration, for some, and fitting felicitations exchanged, though not of the usual protraction, for all had an eye on the cold inclement weather that boded. So, the people were departing Bailethuama in the other county in diverse directions homewards. As were the people of the place I'm talking about. And they were only middlin' satisfied, if at all. The Bochtáns were never entirely fortunate. An' devil mend them. An' scald them. No matter. What time is it? . . Miss!

Mary   Seven. Eight. (*The tips of her fingers to her forehead.*)

Mommo   I'm waiting for someone. Supa tea.

Mary   It's on the chair beside you.

Mommo   Oh an' he *will* come yet. (*A warning to* **Mary**.) And he has a big stick.

Mary (*remains seated: she knows from experience what the outcome of the conversation is going to be; she does not lift her eyes*)   And time to take your pills.

Mommo (*has no intention of taking them*)   The yellow ones?

Mary   Yes.

Mommo   They're good for me?

Mary   I'll give you a cigarette.

Mommo   They'll help me sleep?

Mary   Yes.

Mommo   Heh heh heh heh.

Mary (*to herself*)   And I'd like to read, Mommo.

Mommo   Now there was a decent man at that market and his decent wife the same. Strangers, strangers! Sure they could have come from the south of – Galway! – for all I know. And they had sold not at all. Well, if you call the one basket of pullets' eggs valiant trade. (*She takes a sip of the tea.*) Too hot. No. Their main cargo which consisted of eighteen snow-white geese still lay trussed in the floor of the cart, 'gus bhár ar an mi-ádh sin (*and to make matters worse*) the pitch on an incline of the road was proving an impossibility for the horse to surmount. But he was a decent man, and he took not belt – nor the buckle-end of it as another would – to the noble animal that is the horse. Put it down! (*The last to* **Mary** *who is standing by having put a little more milk into* **Mommo***'s tea.*) No. But spoke only in the gentlest of terms, encouraging the poor beast to try once more against the adversary. 'Try again, Pedlar.' For that was the horse's name. Is that a step?

Mary (*listening*)   . . . Dolly was to call last night. (*The sound they have heard – if any – does not materialise further.*) Nobody. She didn't call the night before either.

Mommo   What's this?

Mary *does not understand.*

Taking down the good cup!

Mary   It tastes nicer out of a –

Mommo   Mug, a mug! – oh leave it so now! Put it down!

Mary   And nicer to have your pills with.

Mommo   The yellow ones? – Try again, Pedlar, for-that-was-the-horse's name!

Mary *returns to the table.*

And all the while his decent wife on the grass verge and she cráite (*crestfallen*). And a detail which you may contemplate fondly now but was only further testimonial to the misfortunes of that unhappy couple, each time she went to draw the shawl more tightly round her frailty, the hand peepin' out held three sticks of rock. Now! Yis, gifts for her care, three small waiting grandchildren. Like ye. Isn't it a good one? (*A sip of tea.*) Cold.

Mary (*to herself*)   I can't stand it.

But she is up again in a moment to add a little hot water and a little more sugar to the tea.

Mommo   And she up to the fifty mark!

Mary (*to herself*)   And that bitch Dolly.

Mommo   Or was she maybe more?

Mary   In heat again.

Mommo   And what was her husband? Decorous efficiency in all he cared to turn his hand to, like all small men. Sure he had topped the sixty!

Mary   Taste that and see if it's alright for you.

Mommo   But he was unlucky. He was. He was. An' times, maybe, she was unkind to him. (*Childlike.*) Was she?

Mary   No. (*Returning to the table where she sits, her head back on her shoulders, looking up at the ceiling.*)

Mommo   And how many children had she bore herself?

Mary   Eight?

Mommo   And what happened to them?

Mary   Nine? Ten?

Mommo   Hah?

Mary   What happened us all?

Mommo   Them (*that*) weren't drowned or died they said she drove away.

Mary   Mommo?

Mommo   Let them say what they like.

Mary   I'm very happy here.

Mommo   Hmmph!

Mary   I'm Mary.

Mommo   Oh but she looked after her grandchildren.

Mary   Mommo?

Mommo   Tom is in Galway. He's afeared of the gander.

Mary   But I'm so . . . (*She leaves it unfinished, she can't find the word.*)

Mommo   To continue.

Mary   Please stop. (*She rises slowly.*)

Mommo   Now man and horse, though God knows they tried, could see the icy hill was not for yielding.

Mary   Because I'm so lonely.

She puts on her apron mechanically, then sets to work. Progressively working harder: scrubbing that part of the floor **Mommo** *has spat upon, clearing away and washing up the crockery, washing clothes that have been soaking in a bucket . . . Later in the play, working, working: sheets to be put soaking in a bucket overnight, bringing in the turf . . .*

Mommo   So what was there for doing but to retrace the hard-won steps to the butt-end of the road which, as

matters would have it, was a fork. One road leading up the
incline whence they came, the other to Bochtán.

Now that man knew that the road to Bochtán, though of
circularity, was another means home. And it looked level
enough stretching out into the gathering duskess. And
'deed he knew men from his own village (*who*) had
travelled it and got home safe and sound. Still he paused.
Oh not through fear, for if he was a man to submit he
would've threwn himself into the river years ago. No. But
in gentleness, sad the searching eye on the road. And
sadder still the same grey eyes were growing in
handsomeness as the years went by. She had noted it. But
she'd never comment on this becoming aspect of his mien
for, strange, it saddened her too. It did. But the two little
smiles appearing, one each side of his mouth, before taking
a step anywhere. Even when only to go to the back door
last thing at night an' call in the old dog to the hearth.

*Mary hears the 'putt-putt' of a motorcycle approaching, stopping
outside.*

Mary   Right!

Suggesting she is going to have matters out with **Dolly**. **Dolly**
*comes in. Like her name, dolled-up, gaudy rural fashion. She is
carrying a crash-helmet. She is thirty-nine.* **Mommo** *is paused in
her own thoughts and does not notice* **Dolly**'s *entrance;* **Mary** *does
not acknowledge it, she has resumed working.* **Dolly** *remains with
her back to the front door for some time.*

Mommo   Last thing at night . . . An' then the silence,
save the tick of the clock . . . An' why didn't she break it?
She knew how to use the weapon of silence. But why didn't
he? A woman isn't stick or stone. The gap in the bed,
concern for the morrow, how to keep the one foot in front
of the other. An' when would it all stop .   What was the
dog's name? (*Childlike.*) D'ye know I can't remember.

Dolly   Mo Dhuine.

Mommo   Shep, was it?

Dolly   Mo Dhuine.

Mommo   Spot? Rover? Mo Dhuine! Mo Dhuine! Now!
Mo Dhuine.

Dolly   Jesus.

Mommo   He loved Mo Dhuine – Ahona ho gus ha-haa!
– An' the bother an' the care on him one time filling the
eggshell with the hot ember an' leavin' it there by the
door.

Dolly   Then the root in the arse –

Mommo   Then the root in the arse to poor Mo Dhuine,
the twig 'cross his back, to get along with him an' the
mouth burned in him! Oh but it did, *did*, cured him of
thievin' the eggs.

Dolly *switches on the light.*

Mommo*'s eyes to the light bulb.*

Dolly   What're yeh doin' workin' in the dark?

Mommo   But they had to get home.

Dolly   Oh, she can't have everything her own way.

Mommo   Their inheritance, the three small waiting
children, left unattended.

Dolly (*rooting in her bag, producing a bottle of vodka*)   How
yeh!

Mary *merely nods, continues working.*

Mommo   And night fast closing around them.

Dolly   Stronger she's gettin'. A present.

Mary (*hopeful that the vodka is for her birthday*)   For what?

Dolly   'Cause I couldn't come up last night.

Mary   What do I! (*want with a bottle of vodka*)

Dolly   Yeh never know. She'll last forever.

Mommo   Then, drawing a deep breath. (*She draws a deep breath.*) Oh but didn't give vent to it, for like the man he was I'm sayin', refusing to *sigh* or submit. An', 'On we go, Pedlar' says he, an' man, horse, cart, and the woman falling in 'tween the two hind shafts set off on the road to Bochtán which place did not come by its present appellation, Bailegangaire, till that very night. Now.

Dolly   Jesus, Bailegangaire – D'yeh want a fag? – night after night, can't you stop her? A fag?

Mary (*declines the cigarette*)   No.

Dolly   Night after night the same old story – (*Proffering cigarettes again.*) Ary you might as well.

Mary *ignores her*.

By Jesus I'd stop her.

Mary   I wish you'd stop using that word, Dolly. I've been trying to stop her.

Dolly   Michaeleen is sick. The tonsils again. So I couldn't come up last night. I'm worried about them tonsils. What d'yeh think? So I can't stay long tonight either.

Mary *sighs*.

Mommo   But to come to Bailegangaire so ye'll have it all.

Mary   Aren't you going to say hello to her?

Dolly   What's up with yeh?

Mommo   Them from that place had been to the market were 'riving back home.

Dolly   *Home*, I'm goin'.

Mommo   One of them, Séamus Costello by name.

Mary   Aren't you going to take off your coat?

Dolly   What do you mean?

Mommo   Oh a fine strappin' man.

Mary   What do you mean what do I mean!

Dolly *turns stubbornly into the fire.*

Mommo   Wherever he got it from. The size an' the breadth of him, you'd near have to step into the verge to give him sufficient right-of-way. 'Twould be no use him extending the civility 'cause you'd hardly get around him I'm saying. And he was liked. Rabbits he was interested in. This to his widowed mother's dismay, but that's another thing. And the kind of man that when people'd espy him approaching the gurgle'd be already startin' in their mouths – 'Och-haw'. For he was the exception, ye understand, with humour in him as big as himself. And I'm thinkin' he was the one an' only boast they ever had in that cursèd place. What time is it?

Mary ⎱   Eight.
Dolly ⎰   Nine.

They look at each other and bygones are bygones.

Mary   Quarter past eight.

Mommo   Quarter past eight, an' sure that's not late. That's a rhyme. Now for ye! (*She takes a sip of tea.*) Too sweet.

Mary *rectifying the tea situation. A cajoling tone coming into* **Dolly***'s voice – there is something on her mind, and she is watching and assessing* **Mary** *privately.*

Dolly   They say it's easier to do it for someone else's (*to take care of a stranger*). (*Declining tea which* **Mary** *offers.*) No thanks. And that old story is only upsetting her, Mary. Isn't it?

Mary *is too intelligent to be taken in by* **Dolly***'s tone or tactics – but this is not at issue here: she has other things on her mind. She sits by the fire with* **Dolly** *and now accepts the cigarette.* **Mommo** *is sipping tea.*

Harping on misery, and only wearing herself out. And you. Amn't I right, Mary? And she never finishes it – Why doesn't she finish it? And have done with it. For God's sake.

Mary *considers this ('Finish it? And have done with it.'), then forgets it for the moment. She is just looking into the fire.*

Mary   I want to have a talk to you, Dolly.

Dolly (*cautiously*)   About what?

Mary   Do you remember . . . (*She shakes her head: she does not know.*)

Dolly   What? . . . I know it affects you: Like, her not reco'nisin' you ever – Why wouldn't it? But you were away a long time.

Mary *looks up: she has been only half listening.*

That's the reason.

Mary   . . . I've often thought . . . (*Just looking at the fire again.*)

Dolly   What?

Mary   I may have been too – bossy, at first.

Dolly   Well, well, there could be something in that, too.

Mary   But I wanted to . . . bring about change. Comfort, civilized.

Dolly   Yes, well, but. Though I don't know. You were away an awful long time. I was left holdin' the can. Like, when yeh think of it, you owe me a very big debt.

Mary (*looks up*)   Hmm: A very big?

Dolly   I mean that's why she reco'nises me.

Mary *looking at the fire again;* **Dolly** *watching* **Mary**. *Something on* **Dolly**'s *mind; she coughs in preparation to speak* –

Mary   We had a pony and trap once. The Sunday outings. You don't remember?

Dolly, *puzzled, shakes her head.*

Ribbons. Grandad would always bring ribbons home for our hair. You don't remember.

Dolly   . . . You work too hard.

Mary *laughs to herself at the remark.*

Dolly (*laughs*)   What?

Mary *shakes her head, 'it doesn't matter'.*

Dolly   And you're too serious.

Mary   Do you remember Daddy?

Dolly   Well, the photographs.

They glance at the framed photographs on the wall.

Aul' brown ghosts. (*Playful, but cajoling.*) Y'are, y'are, too serious.

Mary (*eyes back to the fire*)   I suppose I am. I don't know what I'm trying to say. (*Sighs.*) Home.

Mommo (*has put down her cup*)   And that, too, is well.

Dolly   What?

Mary, *another slight shake of her head: she doesn't know.*

Mommo   And now with his old jiggler of a bicycle set again' the gable, Costello was goin' in to John Mah'ny's, the one and only shop for everything for miles around. 'Cold enough for ye, ladies!' Now! Cold enough for ye, ladies. And that was the first remark he was to utter that evening. And the two women he had thus accosted set to gurgling at once and together. 'Caw och-caw, Seamusheen a wockeen, God bless yeh, och-caw,' says the old crone that was in it buyin' the salt. And, 'Uck-uck-uck, uck-uck hunuka huckina-caw, Costello' from the young buxom woman tendin' the shop end of the counter, and she turnin' one of the babes in her arms so that he too could behold the hero. 'Aren't they gettin' awful big, God bless them,' then saying Costello of the two twins an' they gogglin' at him. 'Jack Frost is coming with a vengeance for ye tonight,' says he, 'or the Bogey Man maybe bejingoes'. And to the four or five others now holding tight their mother's apron, 'Well, someone is comin' anyways,' says he, 'if ye all aren't good'. An' then off with him to the end where the drink was.

Dolly   Good man Josie!

Mary   No!

Mommo ⎫ 'Good man, Josie!'
Mary ⎭ Don't encourage her.

Mommo ⎫ Now!
Mary ⎭ I'm –! (*going out of my mind*).

Mommo ⎫ Good man, Josie.
Mary ⎭ I'm trying to stop it!

Mommo ⎫ And that was the second greeting he uttered
⎪ that night.
Mary ⎬ Talk to her!
Dolly ⎭ That's what I try to do!

Mommo   He got no reply.

Dolly (*going to* **Mommo**, *under her breath*)   Good man Josie, Jesus!

Mommo   Nor did he expect one.

Dolly (*calling back to* **Mary**)   And I'm going at quarter to nine! – Good man, Mommo, how's it cuttin'?

Mommo   Good man –! Pardon?

Dolly   How's the adversary treatin' yeh?

Mommo (*to herself*)   Good man Mommo?

Dolly   I brought yeh sweets.

Mommo   There's nothing wrong with me.

Dolly   I didn't say there was.

Mommo   An' I never done nothin' wrong.

Dolly   Sweets!

Mary   Butterscotch, isn't it, Dolly?

Mommo (*to herself, puzzled again*)   Good man – *Who?*

Dolly   Butterscotch, I've oceans of money.

Mary   Your favourites.

Dolly   You like them ones.

Mary   Try one. You (**Dolly**) give it to her.

Mommo   Do I like them ones?

Mary   Suck it slowly.

Dolly   Gob-stoppers I should have brought her.

Mary   Shh!

Dolly   You're lookin' fantastic. (*Going back to the fire.*) It'd be a blessing if she went.

Mary (*placatory*)   Shh, don't say things like (*that*). Talk to her, come on.

Dolly   About what? It's like an oven in here – and I don't understand a word she's sayin'.

Mary   Take off your – (*coat*).

Dolly   I – don't – want – to – take – off – my!

Mary   Tell her about the children.

Dolly   Scafóid, nonsense talk about forty years ago –

Mary   Come on –

Dolly   And I've enough problems of my own. Why don't you stick her in there? (*One of the other rooms.*)

Mary   It's damp. And she understands – recognises you a lot of the time.

Dolly *rolling her eyes but following* **Mary** *back to the bed again.*

Where she can see you.

Dolly Well, the children are all fine, Mommo. (*A slip*) Well, Michaeleen is sick, the tonsils again. I've rubber-backed lino in all the bedrooms now, the Honda is going like a bomb and the *lounge*, my dear, is carpeted. I seen the lean and lanky May Glynn, who never comes near ye or this house, in her garden when I was motoring over but she went in without a salute. I must have distemper too or whatever. Conor, that other lean and lanky bastard, is now snaking his fence in another six inches, and my darlin' mother-in-law, old sharp-eyes-and-the-family rosary, sends her pers'nal blessings to ye both.

Mary Is she babysitting for you?

Dolly No. She is not babysitting for me. (I don't want her or any of the McGrath clan in my house.)

Mommo (*sucking the sweet*) They're nice.

Dolly An' the cat had kittens. (*To* **Mary**.) D'yeh want a kitten? Do you, Mommo? (*A touch of sour, introversion.*) Does anyone? Before I drown them.

Mommo Tom is in Galway.

Mary Did you hear from Stephen?

Dolly The 'wire' again on Friday, regular as clockwork.

Mary Did you hear, Mommo?

Mommo I did. But she told May Glynn not to be waitin', her own mother'd be needin' her, and that they'd be home before dark for sure.

Dolly Eighty-five quid a week and never a line.

Mary He's busy.

Dolly Fuck him. I don't know what to do with the money! (*Sudden introspection again.*) Or do I? I've started saving for a purpose. (*Then impetuously:*) Do *you* want some? Well, do you, Mommo? To go dancin'.

Mary *is laughing at her sister's personality.*

Mary   Stephen will be home as usual for Christmas.

Dolly   For his goose.

Mary   Won't he, Mommo?

Mommo (*to herself*)   Stephen, yes, fugum.

They laugh. Then, **Dolly** *grimly:*

Dolly   Well maybe it'd be better if the bold Stephen skipped his visit home this Christmas. (*Rises and turns her back on them.*) Jesus, misfortunes.

Mary *now wondering, concerned, her eyes on* **Dolly**'*s back, the stout figure.*

Mommo (*to herself*)   Yes. Misfortunes.

Mary   Dolly?

Dolly   Ooh, a cake, a candle – candles! what's the occasion? (*She gives a kiss to* **Mommo**.) Well, I'm off now, darlin', an' God an' all his holy saints protect an' bless yeh.

Mommo (*buried in her own thoughts until now*)   When did you arrive?

Dolly   What?

Mommo   When did you arrive?

Dolly   I arrived –

Mommo   Sure you're welcome, when did you arrive?

Dolly   I arrived –

Mommo   Well did yeh?

Dolly   I did.

Mommo   From where?

Dolly   From –

Mommo   Now. And is that where y'are now?

Dolly   The very location.

Mommo   Now! I never knew that. Where?

Dolly   Ahm . . . Aw Jesus, Mommo, you have us all as confused as yourself! Ballindine. Ball-in-dine.

Mommo   Hah? Oh yes, yeh told me. Now. Who are you?

Dolly   Dolly, I think.

Mommo (*considering this, sucking her sweet*)   Now. Dolly.

Dolly   Dolly!

Mommo   Yes.

Dolly   Look, I have to be – (*going*)   I'm Dolly, your granddaughter, and that's Mary, your other granddaughter, and your grandson Tom, Tom is dead.

Mary   Shh!

Dolly   Ar, shh! (*To* **Mommo**.) Now do you know?

Mommo   I do. I'm waiting for someone.

Dolly   Who're yeh waiting for?

Mommo   I'm not tellin' yeh.

Dolly   A man, is it?

Mommo (*laughing*)   'Tis.

Dolly   Ahona ho gus hah-haa, an' what'll he have for yeh!

Mommo (*laughing*)   A big stick.

Dolly   M-m-m-m-m! – A big stick, the bata! Mmmah! (*Sexual innuendo.*)   Now! Try that subject on her if you want to stop her.

Mommo   Oh but they were always after me.

Dolly   An' did they ketch yeh?

Mommo   The ones I wanted to.

Dolly   An' are they still after yeh?

Mommo   But I bolt the door – on some of them. (*Laughing.*)

Dolly (*to* **Mary**)   That's what all the aul ones like to talk about. I think you're goin' soft in the head.

Mommo (*recognising her*)   Is it Dolly? Aw is it my Dolly! Well, d'yeh know I didn't rec'nise yeh. Sure you were always the joker. Aw, my Dolly, Dolly, Dolly, come 'ere to me!

Dolly *hesitates, is reluctant, then succumbs to the embrace; indeed, after a moment she is clinging tightly to the old woman.*

Mary *stands by, isolated, watching the scene. She would love to be included. The smallest gesture of affection or recognition would help greatly.*

Ah, lovee. Lovee, lovee, lovee. Sure if I knew you were comin' – (*Aside to* **Mary**.) Will you put on the kettle, will you? Standing there! – I'd've baked a cake. That's an old one. Oh, mo pheata (*my pet*). Why didn't you send word? An' you got fat. You did! On me oath! Will you put on the kettle, Miss, will you! (*Whispering.*) Who is that woman?

Dolly (*tearfully, but trying to joke*)   She's the sly one.

Mommo   She is. (*Loudly, hypocritically.*) Isn't she nice?

Dolly   Watch her.

Mary *goes off to another room.*

Mommo   Why is she interfering?

Dolly   Shh, Mommo.

Mommo   Be careful of that one.

Dolly   Shh, Mommo, I'm in terrible trouble.

Mommo   Yes, watch her.

Dolly (*extricating herself from the embrace, brushing away a tear*)   Leave her to me. I'll deal with her. (*Calls.*) Miss!

Will you come out, will you, an' make a brew! An' put
something in it! Sure you should know about all kinds of
potions.

Mary *has returned with a suitcase. She places it somewhere.*

. . . Someone going on a *voyage*?

Mary   I have to come to a decision, Dolly.

Dolly   Again?

Mary   She's your responsibility too.

Dolly   I know you think I inveigled you back here so that
Stephen and I could escape.

Mary   No one inveigled me anywhere. You're not pulling
your weight.

Dolly (*shrugs*)   There's always the County Home.

Mary   You –

Dolly   Wouldn't I? Why should I stick myself again back
in here?

Mary   Why should I?

Dolly   In a place like this.

Mary   Why do I? In a place like this.

Dolly (*shrugs*)   That's your business. Well, I have to be
going.

Mary   I'd like to go out sometimes too.

Dolly   *Home*, I'm going.

Mary   You look it.

Dolly   Alright, I'll tell you, so that you can go, where the
man is waiting.

Mary   Man? *Men!*

Dolly *shrugs, is moving off.*

I need to talk to – *someone*!

Dolly (*her back to* **Mary**; *quietly*)   I need to talk to someone too.

Mary (*an insinuation*)   Why don't you take off your coat?

Dolly (*faces* **Mary**; *a single solemn nod of her head; then*)   Because, now, I am about to leave. I'll figure out something. I might even call back in a while, 'cause it doesn't take long, does it? Just a few minutes; that's all it takes.

Mary   You're disgusting.

Dolly   Am I?

Mary (*going to one of the other rooms*)   I've *come* to a decision. (*Off.*) County Home! You won't blackmail me!

Dolly (*to herself*)   I hate this house. (*To* **Mommo**.) Good man Josie! (*Going out; an undertone.*) Ah, fuck it all.

Mommo   Oh yes. 'Good man, Josie!' Now! Good man Josie. And that was the second greeting Costello was to utter that evening.

Mary (*coming in*)   I'll leave everything here for you spic and span, of course.

She has not heard **Dolly** *go out; now she stands there looking at the door, the motorcycle outside driving away, arms outstretched, her hands clapping together some of her wardrobe (as if demonstrating the possibility that she is leaving rather than confirming it).*

Mommo   He got no reply. Nor did he expect one. For Josie was a Greaney and none was ever right in that fambly. An' the threadbare fashion'ry, not a top-coat to him, the shirt neck open.

Mary (*to herself*)   Not a gansey.

Mommo   Nor a gansey.

Mary   *Nor* a gansey.

Mommo   An' the tuthree raggedy top-coats on the others.

Mary   It's not fair. (*To herself.*)

Mommo   Though some say he had the knack of mendin' clocks, if he had.

Mary (*angrily: still to the door*)   Stephen? *Your* Stephen?! It was *me* he wanted! ('But I told him: keep off!') That's why he took *you*!

Mommo (*she has had a sip of tea*)   What's in this? Miss!

Mary   The County Home! (*Gesturing, meaning did* **Mommo** *hear what* **Dolly** *said.*)

Mommo   Hot drink, decent supa tea!

Mary (*automatically sets about making fresh tea, then she stops*)   I have *come* to a decision I said! Do you understand? So if you could wait a moment. (*She starts to discard some of the clothes, packing others; talking to herself again.*) Just to see who is in earnest this time.

Mommo   Me mouth is dry d'ye know.

Mary   And I was doing well – I was the success! Now I'm talking to myself. And I *will* leave the place spic and span.

Mommo   Howandever. 'How the boys!' was Costello's third greeting. This time to two old men with their heads in the fire. The one of them givin' out the odd sigh, smoking his pipe with assiduity and beating the slow obsequies of a death-roll with his boot. An' the other, a Brian by name, replying in sagacity 'Oh yis,' sharing the silent mysteries of the world between them. Me mouth is (*dry*), d'ye know.

Mary   Just a moment! (*Going to another room.*) Dependent on a pension and that bitch.

Mommo   Where is she? Miss!

Mary (*off*)   Miss! Miss! Miss is coming! (*Entering with more clothes.*) Miss: as if I didn't exist. That's the thanks I get, that's the − (*Winces to herself.*) It's − not − thanks I'm looking for. (*Absently.*) What am I looking for? I had to come home. No one inveigled me. I wanted to come home.

Mommo   Put it down, put it down!

Mary, *exasperated, comes out of her reverie, dumps the clothes and sets about making more tea.*

Mary   And you know very well who I am! You do! You do!

Mommo   Sure it's often I'd be watchin' me own father engaged in the same practice, drawing wisdom from the fire. 'Deed, on one such occasion, an' twas maybe after a full hour's contemplation, he craned his neck, the glaze to his eyes, to accost me with the philosophy that was troublin' him. 'How much does a seagull weigh?' I held my silence to be sure, for times he'd get cross − oh he'd welt yeh with the stick − if a guess was attempted or a sound itself uttered. For he wouldn't be talkin' to you at all. The groans out of that man decipherin' the enigmal. Then, at last, when he found for himself the answer to the riddle he declared in 'sured solemnity, 'I'm thinking two ounces'. Now! That's who I'm waitin' for. Oh, men have their ways an' women their places an' that is God's plan, my bright ones.

She has got out of bed. **Mary** *sees her and is hurrying to her assistance.*

Shthap!

Mary *is stopped by the ferocity.* **Mommo** *squats, hidden behind the headboard of the bed.*

Mary   . . . And to change your nightdress . . . I was a nurse, Mommo . . . And offers of marriage.

Then, quickly, efficiently, she takes the opportunity of re-making the bed. She replaces the sheets with clean ones, removes the bed-warmer

– which is a cast-iron lid of a pot in a knitted woollen cover; she puts the lid into the fire to reheat it. She appears almost happy when she is working constructively. She recites as she works.

'There is the silence of copse or croft
When the wind sinks dumb.
And of belfry loft
When the tenor after tolling stops its hum.'

And sure you have lots of poems, lots of stories, nice stories, instead of that old one. 'Mick Delaney' – Do you remember that one? We loved that one. How did it begin? Or ghost stories. People used to come *miles* to hear you tell stories. Oh! And do you remember: the gramophone? Yes, we had a gramophone too. 'The banshee is out tonight go down (*on*) your knees and say your prayers – Wooooo!' Or would you like me to read you a story?

Mommo (*reappearing from behind the bed*)   Heh heh heh heh!

Mary   Why can't you be civil to me? At least tonight. There was happiness here too, Mommo. Harmony?

Mommo (*straight back, neck craned*)   You can be going now, Miss.

Mary   . . . Alright.

She takes the chamberpot from behind the headboard of the bed and goes out. We can see her outside, motionless; a little later, continuing motionless except for the movements of smoking a cigarette.

Mommo   She knows too much about our business entirely. (*She calls hypocritically.*) And thank you! (*Giggles getting back into the bed.*) Now amn't I able for them?
   But now that Costello was in it the aspect was transforming. 'An',' says old Brian, taking his head out of the fire, 'What's the news from the Big World?' 'The Dutch has taken Holland!' says Costello with such a rumble out of him near had the whole house shook asunder and all in it in ululation so infectious was the sound. Save

Josie who was heedless, but rapping with severity on the counter for more libation. And 'John!' says the young buxom woman, calling to her husband – 'John!' – to come out and tend his end of the counter, an' she now putting questions on bold Costello.

'You wor in Tuam?' says she, 'I was in Tuam,' says he, 'Yeh wor?' says she, 'I was,' says he, 'An' how was it?' says she.

'Well, not tellin' you a word of a lie now,' says he 'but 'twas deadly'.

And 'Ory!' says the crone that was in it buyin' the salt.

'Did yeh hear?' says the young buxom woman to her husband, John, to be sure. He had 'rived from the kitchen an' was frownin' pullin' pints. Merchants d'ye know: good market or bad, the arithmetic in the ledger has to come out correct.

'Well do yeh tell me so?' says the young buxom woman.

'I do tell yeh so,' says Costello. 'Talkin' about a Maragadh Mór? – I never in all me born days seen light or likes of it!'

Now they were listening.

Mary *comes in. She selects her 'going-away' suit. She tries the waist against herself. She puts the suit on a chair beside the fire to air it. Through the following she goes out/comes in with turf for the night.*

Mommo   'Firkins of butter,' says he, 'an' cheese be the hundred-weight. Ducks, geese, chickens, bonavs and – Geese!' says he, 'geese! There was hundreds of them! There was hundreds upon hundreds of thousands of them! The ground I tell ye was white with them!'

And 'White with them,' says the crone.

'They went ch-cheap then?' says John, still bowed frownin' over the tricks of pullin' porter.

'Cheap then?' says Costello, 'sure yeh couldn't give them away sure. Sure the sight of so many chickens an' geese an'! Sure all the people could do was stand and stare.'

'They were puzzled,' says the crone.

'I'm tellin' ye,' says Costello, 'Napoleon Bonaparte

wouldn't have said no to all the provisions goin' a-beggin'
in that town of Tuam today.'

An' 'Hah?' says John, squintin', the head-work
interrupted.

'On his retreat from Moscow, sure,' says Costello. 'Or
Josephine – Wuw! – neither.'

Now! Wuw. Them were his ways, an' he having the
others equivalently pursuant: 'Wo ho ho, wo ho ho!'

'But you sis-sold your rabbits, did yeh, Costello?' says
John. An' wasn't there a gap. Oh, only for the second. 'Oh
I sold them,' then sayin' Costello. 'Oh I did, did,' saying
he, 'Oh on me solemn 'n dyin' oath! Every man-jack-
rabbit of them.' Like a man not to be believed, his bona
fides in question.

'Yeh-yeh codjer yeh-yeh,' says John. Whatever he
meant. But he was not at all yet feeling cordial.

But thus was the night faring into its progression, others
'riving back home an' how did they do an' who else was in
it, did they buy e'er a thing, Costello settin' them laughin',
John frownin' an' squintin', an' the thief of a Christmas
they wor all goin' t'have. What're ye doin' there?

Mary *is stacking the turf near the fire. She holds up a sod of turf to
show* **Mommo**.

Hah? . . . There's nothing here for people to be prying in
corners for. Bring in the brishen of turf for the night an'
then you may go home to your own house.

Mary   Alright.

*She moves as if going out back door, then silently to the comparative
dark of the far corner where she remains motionless.*

Mommo   You couldn't be up to them . . . (*She yawns.*)
Oh ho huneo! An' twas round about now the rattlin' of the
horse an' cart was heard abroad on the road an' had them
in the shop peepin' at the windy. 'Twas the decent man
an' his decent wife the same was in it. And 'Stand, Pedlar,'
says the man in (*a*) class of awesome whisper. And his
decent wife from the heel of the cart to his side to view the

spectre was now before them. The aspect silver of moon an' stars reflecting off the new impossibility. Loughran's Hill. Creature. She now clutching more tightly the sweets to her breast. (*She yawns again: her eyes close.*)

Mary (*whispers*)   Sleep.

Mommo (*eyes open*)   Hah? *Now* what was there for doing? Which way to cast the hopeful eye? No-no, not yet, in deliberate caution, would he acknowledge the shop, John Mah'ny's, forninst them, but looked behind him the road they came, forward again, but to what avail? There was only John Mah'ny's now for his contemplation, nature all around them serenely waiting, and didn't the two little smiles come appearing again.

Mary (*whispers*)   Sleep.

Mommo   Hah?

Mary   Sleep, sleep, peace, peace.

Mommo   An' the strangers, that decent man an' his decent wife the same, rounded the gable into the merchant's yard, an' sorry the night that was the decision. What time is it? . . . She's gone. An' she can stay gone. But them are the details, c'rrect to the particular. And they can be vouched for. For there was to be many's the inquisition by c'roner, civic guard and civilian on all that transpired in John Mah'ny's that night. Now. (*She yawns:*) Wasn't that a nice story? An' we'll all be goin' to sleep.

She is asleep.

Tommy O'Brien's programme is over (or nearly over): it is followed by an announcement of what The Sunday Concert is going to be later on: 'A Shubert Evening, Symphony No. 9, 'The Great', followed by 'Notturno' in E Flat. But now we have Archives *presented by . . .' etc.*

Mary (*looking at* **Mommo**)   Sleep?

For how long? . . .

She switches off the radio. She switches off the light. She goes to the table and idly starts lighting candles on the cake, using a new match to light each one. A car passes by outside. She blows out the candles, tires of them. Now what to do? . . .

(*Idly at first:*) Now as all do know the world over . . . Now as all do know . . . Now as all do know the world over the custom when entering the house of another – be the house public, private with credentials or no – is to invoke our Maker's benediction on all present. (*Adds a piece of sardonic humour:*) Save the cat. Well, as the Bochtán-Bailegangaires would have it later, no mention of our Maker, or His Blessed Son, was mentioned by the strangers as they came 'cross John Mahoney's threshel (*threshold*) that night. But no, no, no, no, no. No now! They were wrongin' that couple. (*To the sleeping* **Mommo**.) Weren't they? They were. They wor. (*To* **Mommo**.) And when you. And when that decent woman gave the whole story to her father, what did he say? (*A touch of mimicry of* **Mommo**.) An' believe you me he knew all about them. That them Bochtán-Bailegangaires were a venomous pack of jolter-headed gobshites. Didn't he? He did. An ill-bred band of amadáns an' oinseachs, untutored in science, philosophy or the fundamental rudimentaries of elementary husbandry itself. A low crew of illiterate plebs, drunkards and incestuous bastards, and would ever continue as such, improper and despicable in their incorrigibility. Them were his words. Weren't they? They wor. They're not nice, he said. Supa tea. (*She pours a glass of vodka for herself.*) And he was the man to give the tongue-lashin'. An' 'twas from him I got my learnin'. Wasn't it? That's who I'm waitin' for. (*She has a sip of the vodka.*) Too sweet. (*She dilutes the vodka with water.*) Me father. He has a big stick. That's where security lies. (*She has a drink: then, whimpering as* **Mommo** *might.*) I wanta go home, I wanta go home. (*New tone, her own, frustrated.*) So do I, so do I. *Home.* (*Anger.*) Where is it, Mommo?

Then she is sorry for her anger. She pulls herself together for a few moments. The silence is now being punctuated by another car passing by outside.

A lot of activity tonight. And all weekend.

Mary *picks up her book and does not open it. She starts to pace the periphery of the room.*

'There is the silence of copse or croft
When the wind sinks dumb.
And of belfry loft
When the tenor after tolling stops its hum.

And there's the silence of a lonely pond
Where a man was drowned . . .'

She stops for a moment or two looking at one of the framed photographs.

Where a man, and his brother who went to save him were drowned. Bury them in pairs, it's cheaper.

Continues pacing.

'Nor nigh nor yond
No newt, toad, frog to make the smallest sound.

But the silence of an empty house
Where oneself was born,
Dwelt, held carouse . . .'

Did we? Hold carouse.

'With friends
Is of all silence most forlorn.

It seems no power can waken it −'

Another car passes by. **Mary***'s reaction to the car:*

Come in! . . . 'It seems no power can waken it,
Or rouse its rooms,
Or the past permit
The present to stir a torpor like a tomb's.'

Bla bla bla bla bla like a tomb's. (*To the book, and dumping it.*) Is that so? Well, I don't agree with you . . . What time is it? Twenty past nine . . . Going crazy. (*Then, on reflection.*) No I'm not. (*Then suddenly to* **Mommo**.) Wake

up *now*, Mommo. Mommo! Because I don't want to wait
till midnight, or one or two or three o'clock in the
morning, for more of your – unfinished symphony. I'm
ready *now*. (*She switches on the light.*) Mommo, the curséd
paraffin! (*She switches on the radio.*) What else did your
father say when you gave him the story? (**Mommo** *is*
awake.) What about the snails? What about the earwigs?

Mommo   'Oh never step on a snail,' he intoned.

Mary   'Nor upon the silver trail he leaves behind.'

Mommo   'For your boot is unworthy.'

Mary   Now!

Mommo   'For the snail knows his place, and understands
the parameters – and the need for parameters – in the case
under consideration, God's prize piece, the earth.'

Mary   Now for yeh!

Mommo   'D'yeh consider,' says me father – the fierce
eyes of that man rolling – 'that God designed all this for
the likes of the gobshite Bochtáns and their antics?'

Mary   Or for the likes of ourselves!

Mommo   Or for the likes of ourselves.

Mary   On with the story! But that decent man and his
decent wife the same did as was proper on entering John
Mahoney's.

Mommo   Sure we weren't meant to be here at all!

Mary   The customary salutation was given.

Mommo   That was one of God's errors.

Mary   Though silently – (*Whispers.*) 'God save all here' –
for they were shy people, and confused in their quandry.
Mommo? And then, without fuss, the man indicated a seat
in the most private corner.

Mommo   An' they were wrongin' them there again! So they wor.

Mary   They were.

Mommo   The whispers bein' exchanged were *not* of malevolent disposition. Yis! – to be sure! – that woman! – Maybe! – had a distracted look to her. Hadn't she reason?

Mary   The Bailegangaires gawpin' at them.

Mommo   They knew no better.

Mary   Where would they learn it?

Mommo   Oh-ho, but he bet them, he bet the best of them! (*Absently asking.*) Cigarette. 'An' I caught Tom playin' with the mangler the other evenin', his feet dancin' in the cup.' That's what she was whisperin'. And he lookin' round, 'Not at all, not at all,' tryin' to look pleasant in the house of another. 'An' won't they have to light the lamp?' That's what she was whisperin'. 'Not at all, not at all,' still lookin' for the place to put his eyes. 'Isn't Mary a big girl now an' well able to look after them.' That's what he was whisperin'. 'An' won't May Glynn be lookin' in on them.' That's what he was whisperin'. But she'd told May Glynn that mornin' not to be waitin', her mother'd be needin' her to look after her young brothers, an' they'd be home before dark for sure. And-sure-she-was-gettin'-on-his-nerves! Till he had to go an' leave her there to a quiet spot at the counter . . . Sure she should've known better. An' she's sorry now. She is. She is.

She's beginning to whimper, puffing on the cigarette **Mary** *has given her.*

Mary *coming to comfort her.*

Shtap! . . . (*Whimpering.*) I wanta go home. I wanta see mah father. (*Warning* **Mary**.) And he has a big stick. And he wont try to stop me.

Mary (*thoughtfully, to herself*)   . . . No, I'm not trying to stop you, 'Why doesn't she finish it and have done with it.' (*A* **Dolly** *line from earlier.*)

Mommo   Heh heh heh heh! (*She then winks wisely at the imagined children at the foot of the bed.*) Men long-married to tearful women are no use to them, my bright ones. But are apt to get cross, and make matters worse, when they can't see the solution. (*She becomes conscious of the cigarette.*) What's this? An' who asked for this?

Mary (*taking cigarette from her*)   I'm not stopping you. And I just had an idea.

Mommo   Me mouth is burned.

Mary   We'll finish it – We'll do it together.

Mommo   Rubbishy cigarettes – spendin' money on rubbishy cigarettes –

Mary   I'm not stopping you.

Mommo (*singing: her defiance to* **Mary**)   'Once I loved with fond affection –'

Mary   And if we finished it, that would be something, wouldn't it? –

Mommo   'All my thoughts they were in thee' –

Mary   Wouldn't it? –

Mommo   'Till a dark-haired girl deceived me, And no more he thought of me.' (*She lapses into silence, she grows drowsy, or feigns drowsiness.*)

Mary   Don't go to sleep, and don't be pretending to sleep either. . . . I'll help you, Mommo. And what'll you be havin', says John Mahony the proprietor. But the stranger was now taking in the laughter and Costello's great bellow dominating over all.
    'A lotta noise an' little wool as the devil says shearin' the pig!' sayin' Costello. Wo ho ho! 'An what'll you be havin', Mister,' says John Mahony again. 'A little drop of whiskey

an' a small port wine.' And readying the drinks, says John, 'The frost is determined to make a night of it?'

'Behell I don't know,' says old Brian, like the nestor long ago, 'comin' on duskess there was a fine roll of cloud over in the west and if you got the bit of a breeze at all I'm thinkin' you'd soon see a thaw.' And the stranger had produced his purse and was suspended-paused takin' in the forecast. But the two little smiles appearing again: such good fortune as a thaw was not to be. Then – and with a deft enough flick – he pitched the coin on the counter – like a man rejecting all fortune. Good enough.

He took the drink to his decent wife and was for sitting next to her again but wasn't her head now in and out of the corner and she startin' the cryin'.

Mommo   She should have known better.

Mary   So what could he do but leave her there again?

Mommo   An' the church owed him money.

Mary   Did it?

Mommo (*growls*)   The-church-owed-him-money. Oh, the church is slow to pay out, but if you're givin', there's nothin' like money to make the clergy fervent.

Mary   Yes?

Mommo (*drowsily*)   And I'm thinkin' that decent man of late was given to reviewin' the transpirations since his birth . . . But if he was itself, wasn't his decent wife the same? . . . At the end of her tether . . . They were acquainted with grief. They wor . . . Switch off that aul' thing there's nothing on it. (*The radio.*) . . . They wor.

Mary (*has turned the volume down*)   Mommo? I know you're pretending.

The silence again.

They were acquainted with grief . . . Alright, I won't just help you, I'll do it for you. (*Progressively she begins to dramatise the story.*) Now John Mahony – (*She corrects her pronunciation*.) Now John Mah'ny – was noticing the goings-on between the two and being the proprietor he was possessed of the licence for interrogating newses. And 'You have a d-distance teh-teh go, Mister?' says he at the stranger. An' says Grandad. An' says the stranger, class of frownin': 'Would that big man down there, be a man by the name of Costello?' And, 'Th-that's who he is,' says John, 'd'yeh know him?' 'No,' says the stranger, in curious introspection, an' 'No' says he again – *still* puzzled in the head. 'But that's a fine laugh.' 'Oh 'tis a f-fine laugh right enough,' says John, 'hah?' Knowin' more was comin' but hadn't yet reached the senses. And the stranger now drawin' curlicues with his glass upon the counter! Then says he, 'I heard that laugh a wintry day two years ago across the market square in Ballindine an' I had t'ask a man who he was.' 'Yeh had,' says John, 'I had,' says the stranger. An' John was in suspense. And then of a suddenness didn't the frown go disappearin' up the stranger's cap. He had it at last. 'Well,' says he – Oh, lookin' the merchant between the two eyes, 'Well,' says he, 'I'm a better laugher than your Costello.'

What time is it? Half-nine. *Someone* will come yet. '*Nother* supa milk (*Short laugh to herself as she gets another glass of vodka*.) Well, I'm a better laugher than your Costello. (*She swallows the drink*.) Now the merchant betrayed nothing. He was well-versed in meeting company, an' all he did was nod the once – (*She nods*.) – and then, quick enough of him, referred the matter. And 'Sh-Sheamus!' says he, 'Sh-sh-Sheamus!' callin' Costello to come down.

She is now listening to the 'putt-putt' of the motorcycle approaching.

A mortal laughing competition there would be.

Mary *now into action, putting away her glass, switching off the radio, getting needle, thread, scissors and the skirt of her 'going-away' suit to take in the waist.*

I knew some one would call. Dolly. Again! I wonder why. (*Cynically*.) Bringing tidings of great joy.

Dolly *comes in. She stretches herself. (She has had sex in ditch, doorway, old shed or wherever.) She takes in the packed suitcase but as usual leaves such baiting topics until it suits her.*

Dolly   I have it all figured out.

Mary   The County Home?

Dolly   Well, maybe nothing as drastic as that. That's a nice suit.

Mary (*does not lift her head from her work*)   Kill her?

Dolly (*a sideways twist of the head – 'Kill her?' – a more feasible suggestion*)   Can I have a drop of this? (*Vodka.*)

Mary   You brought it.

Dolly (*produces two bottles of mixers*)   I forgot the mixers earlier. In my haste. (*She pours two drinks.*) We might as well have a wake, an American wake for yeh.

Mary   Not for me. I had a little one earlier, thank you.

Dolly   You had *two* little ones, (*Puts drink beside* **Mary**.) Vodka and white. It's a long time since I seen you wearing that.

Mary   Saw.

Dolly   What?

Mary   I wore it coming home.

Dolly   Did you have to let out the waist?

Mary   I have to take *in* my things. (*A gesture of invitation.*) You need to talk to someone.

Dolly   Go on: cheers! Since you're off. Are yeh?

Mary (*does not drink, does not look up but lifts her glass and puts it down again*)   Cheers!

Dolly   And it often crossed my mind the years Stephen and I were here with herself. Kill her. And it wouldn't be none of your fancy nurses' potions either. Get them out of bed, the auld reliable, start them walkin'. Walk the heart out of them. No clues left for coroner or Dr Paddy. And that's how many's the one met their Waterloo. What's the matter?

Mary *shakes her head; just when she does not want to, she is about to break into tears.*

. . . What? . . . Joking! . . . I have it all figured out.

Mary *is crying.*

What's the matter?

Mary   Stop it, Dolly.

Dolly   Mary?

Mary   Leave me alone. (*To get away from* **Dolly** *she goes to the radio and switches it on.*)

Dolly   What's the – Why are you . . .? (*She emits a few whimpers.*) Mary?

Mommo (*has woken up*)   What's the plottin' an' whisperin' for?

Dolly   Good man Josie! (*And immediately back to* **Mary** *again.*) What? (*Crying.*) What? . . . Don't. Please. (*Her arms around* **Mary**.)

They are all speaking at once. **Mary** *and* **Dolly** *crying.*

Mommo   Oh yes, 'Good man, Josie.' Now! Good man, Josie. And that was the second greeting he uttered that night.

Dolly   What's the matter? . . . Shh! . . . What?

Mary   I don't know, I don't know.

Mommo   He got no reply. Nor did he expect one. For Josie was a Greaney, an' none was ever right in that fambly.

Mary   I wanted to come home.

Dolly   What?

Mary   I had to come home.

Mommo   An' the threadbare fashion'ry, not a top-coat
to him, the shirt neck open, nor a gansey.

Dolly   What?

Mary   This is our home.

Dolly   I know, I know.

Mary   This is *home*?

Dolly   I know it is.

Mary (*pulling away from* **Dolly** *to shout at* **Mommo**)   Finish
it, finish it, that much at least –

Mommo   Heh-heh-heh-heh! (*Defiantly.*)

Mary   Have done with it! – that much at least! (*To*
Dolly *who is following her.*) Why don't you take off your
coat! (*To* **Mommo**.) What was waiting for them at dawn
when they got home in the morning?

Mary's *remark to* **Dolly** *has stopped* **Dolly** *for a moment, but*
Dolly *comes to* **Mary** *and puts her arms around her again, the two
of them crying through to the end. And* **Mommo** *has not given way
to the above: she has started the story again from the beginning.*

Mommo   It was a bad year for the crops, a good one for
mushrooms . . . (*etc.*)

*The lights fading through the above, a car passing by outside and
music up.*

Act Two

An announcement for The Sunday Concert *on the radio together with* **Mommo**'s *voice continuing her story.* **Mommo** *has arrived at and is repeating the last section of the story where* **Mary** *left off in Act One.*

A sniff from **Mary**, *her tears are all but finished. Both she and* **Dolly** *have their 'vodkas and white' and a slice of the birthday cake on plates beside them.* **Mary** *is examining a small computerised gadget.*

Mommo . . . 'Yeh had', says John, 'I had' says the stranger.

Mary What is it? (*The gadget.*)

Dolly I don't know. Happy birthday!

Mommo An' John was in suspense. An' then of a suddenness didn't the frown go disappearing up the stranger's cap. He had it at last.

Mary It's not a calculator.

Dolly Data processing thing from the plant above.

Mary You didn't get a handbook?

Dolly I got it off one of the lads, working in the – You're the brainy one.

Mommo 'Well,' says he – oh lookin' the merchant between the two eyes – 'Well,' says he, 'I'm a better laugher than your Costello.'

Dolly Give it to her if you like.

Mary No. (*It is precious; a present.*) I'm sorry for. (*Crying.*)

A car passes by outside.

Dolly   Ar – Phhh – don't be silly. Did yeh see the
helicopter on Friday? The plant, they say, is for closure.
The Chinese are over.

Mary   Japanese. (*Her attention now returning to* **Mommo**.)

Mommo   Now the merchant betrayed nothing.

Dolly   I prefer to call them Chinese.

Dolly's *mind beginning to tick over on how to present her
'proposition' to* **Mary**. **Mary**'s *nervous energy, after the lull,
setting her to work again, washing her plate, removing the bed-
warmer from the fire and slipping it into the bed at* **Mommo**'s *feet,
wrapping up the cake in tinfoil and putting it away, stoking the
fire . . . but, predominantly, her eyes, concentration, returning to*
Mommo; *a resoluteness increasing to have* **Mommo**'s *story
finished.*

Mommo   He was well-versed at meeting company. And
all he did was nod the once. (*She nods solemnly.*)

Dolly   I must get a set of decent glasses for you the next
time I'm in town.

Mommo   Then, quick enough of him, referred the
matter.

Dolly   And I'm sure there's rats in that thatch.

Mommo   An' 'Sh-Sheamus!' says he.

Dolly   I could see Hallilan the contractor about slatin' it.

Mommo   'Sh-Sheamus!' Calling Costello to come down.

Dolly   What d'yeh think?

Mary   Shhh!

Mommo   A laughing competition there would be.

Dolly (*puzzled by* **Mary**'s *behaviour*)   And I was thinking of
getting her a doll.

Mary   Let's see if she'll continue.

Dolly   What?

Mary   Good enough. Then down steps the bold Costello.

Mommo (*and instead of continuing she starts singing*)   'Once I loved with fond affection, all my thoughts they were in thee, till a dark haired girl deceived me, and no more he thought of me.'

Mary (*through* **Mommo**'s *song, returning to the fire, all the time looking at* **Mommo**)   Down steps the bold Costello – You have a suggestion, something figured out.

Dolly   What?

Mary   She's going to finish it.

Dolly   Finish it? Why?

Mary   I don't know. I can't do anything the way things are.

Mommo   Now. Ye like that one.

Dolly   Sit down. I thought you were trying to stop her.

Mary   She's going to finish it.

Dolly   You're always on your feet –

Mary   *Tonight!*

Dolly   Another drink?

Mary   No. A laughing competition there *will* be! (*And goes to* **Mommo**.) Then down steps the bold Costello.

Mommo   Pardon?

Mary   Then down steps the bold Costello.

Mommo   Oh yes.

Dolly   Well, as a matter of fact, I do have a proposition.

Mary   Shhh!

Mommo   Then down steps the bold Costello. And 'Hah?' says he, seeing the gravity on the proprietor's mien.

But the proprietor – John, to be sure – referred him like
that (*She nods in one direction.*) An 'Hah?' says Costello,
lookin' at the stranger. But weren't the eyes of the stranger
still mildly fixed on John, an' 'Hah?' says Costello, lookin'
back at John. But there was no countin' John's cuteness.
He takes the two steps backwards, then the one to the
sidewards, slidin' his arse along the shelf to 'scape the
strangers line of vision an' demonstrate for all his
neutrality in the matter. 'Hah?' poor Costello goin'. 'Hah?'
to the one, 'Hah?' to the other. 'Hah?' 'Hah?' The head
near swung off his neck, an' now wonderin' I'm sure what
on earth he'd done wrong.

Dolly   Mary? (*Topping up the drinks.*)

Mommo   An' no help from John. Puffing a tuneless
whistle at the ceiling! 'Phuh-phuh-phuh-phuh.' (*John's
tuneless whistle.*)

Mary (*absently accepting drink*)   Phuh-phuh-phuh-phuh.

Dolly (*to herself*)   Jesus!

Mommo   Then says the stranger, lookin' straight ahead
at nothing –

Dolly   She's (**Mary**.) gone loopey too.

Mommo   Though 'twas polite introduction – 'How
d'yeh do, Mr Costello, I'm Seamus O'Toole'. Costello:
'Hah? I'm very well, thanking you!' His face was a study.
An' 'Oh,' says John of Costello, 'he's a Sh-Sheamus too,
phuh-phuh-phuh-phuh.' 'I know that,' says the stranger,
'but I'm a better laugher than 'm.' 'Quawk awk-awk-
awk?' In Costello's throat. In response didn't the stranger
make serious chuckle. And in response didn't Costello roar
out a laugh.

A silent 'Jesus' from **Dolly**. *She decides to take off her coat and see
what effect flaunting her pregnancy will have.*

Mary   Good girl! (*Silently with* **Mommo**.) Then loud as
you please . . . . .

Mommo   Then loud as you please says Costello: 'He says, he says, he says,' says he, 'he's a better.' (*She claps her mouth shut.*) An' that was far as he got. For in the suddenness of a discovery he found out that he was cross.

'Ara phat?' says he – He was nimble? – The full size of him skippin' backwards, the dancing antics of a boxing-man. An' lookin' 'bout at his supporters, now hushed an' on their marks, 'He says, he says, he says,' says he, 'he's a better laugher than me!'

What! Sure they never heard the likes. Nor how on earth to deal with it. An' the upset on their own man's face! – Oh, they wor greatly taken 'back. Oh they wor. An' not up to disseration things wor lookin' dangerous.

Dolly   She's getting tired – the creature.

Mary   Shhh!

Dolly   Cheers!

Mary   Cheers – Things were looking dangerous.

Mommo   Oh, they wor.

Mary   'Ary give me (*a*) pint outa that.'

Mommo   Costello?

Mary *nods*.

Swivellin' an' near knockin' them wor behind him, but then in retraction comes wheelin' back 'round, the head like a donkey's flung up at the ceilin', eyes like a bull-frog's near out the sockets an' the big mouth threwn open. But God bless us an' save us, all the emission was (a) class of a rattle'd put shame to a magpie.

Mary (*silently, excited*)   Shame to a magpie.

Mommo   Now he was humbled, the big head on him hangin', went back to his corner, turned his back on all present. The hump that was on him! Oh his feelin's wor hurted. (*She yawns.*) Oh ho hun-neo.

Mary   Aa no.

Mommo (*insistent*)   Oh ho hun-neo!

Mary   Don't be pretendin', you had a little nap a while ago.

Mommo   Put the sup of milk there for me now for the night.

Mary   I'll get the milk later. And the others, Mommo?

Mommo   Lookin' wildly, one to the other, from their giant to the stranger, none knowin' what to do.

Dolly (*getting the milk*)   Let her settle down.

Mary   But they were vexed.

Mommo   An' they knew it?

Mary *nods agreement and encouragement.*

Oh they knew they were cross. An' strainin' towards the stranger like mastiffs on chains, fit to tear him asunder.

Dolly   And I don't know if you've noticed, Mary, but the turf out there won't last the winter. (*Approaching with the milk.*) Here we are! I'll see to the turf.

Mary (*takes the milk from* **Dolly**)   No milk.

Dolly   What are you at?

Mary   No milk! (*She puts it away.*)

Mommo   And even Josie! – the odd one –

Dolly (*to herself*)   Jesus Josie! –

Mommo   That always stood aloof! even he was infected with the venom (*that*) had entered, an' all of the floor was 'vailable round him he began to walk circles screechin' 'Hackah!' at the stranger.

Dolly   I want to have a talk!

Mary   Later.

Dolly   A plan, a proposition.

Mary   Later.

Mommo   Pardon?

Dolly   I've a little problem of my own.

Mary   I think I've noticed. Go on, Mommo, no one is stopping you.

Mommo   Where's the milk for the night, Miss?

Mary   Then striding to the stranger – Costello: 'Excuse me there now a minute, Mister –'

Dolly   Mary –

Mary   No! No! 'Excuse me there now a minute now –'

Mommo   Pardon?

Mary   'But what did you say to me there a minute ago?' (*Waits for a beat to see if* **Mommo** *will continue.*) . . . 'That you're a better laugher than me, is it?' . . . 'Well, would you care to put a small bet on it?'

Mommo (*suspiciously, but childlike*)   How do you know that?

Mary   Oh, I was told. But I never heard all of the story.

Mommo   Hah? . . . At shurrup (*shut up*) outa that.

Mary   'Well would you care to put a small bet on it?' And 'No', saying the stranger going back to his wife. 'But you're challenging me, challenging me, challenging me, y'are!'

Mommo   'No', saying the stranger. ''twas only a notion,' his eyes on the floor. For why? Foreseeing fatalistic danger. (**Mary** *nods solemnly.*) Then joined the two little smiles cross the width of his mouth which he gave up to the hero as evidence sincere that he was for abnegating. Can yeh go on?

Mary   No. (*Cajoling.*) Can you?

Mommo   Well, Costello was for agreein'? An' for understandin'? But th' others wor all circlin', jostlin', an' pushin' − (*Josie flailin' like a thrasher − eggin' for diversion*) 'He is, he is, challe'gin' yeh, he is!' 'Up Bochtán, up Bochtán, Bochtán forever!' Putting confusion in the head of Costello again. But the stranger − a cute man − headin' for the door, gives (*the*) nod an' wink to Costello so he'd comprehend the better the excitation (*that*) is produced by the abberation of a notion. Then in the fullness of magistrature, 'Attention!' roaring Costello, 'Attention!' roaring he, to declare his verdict was dismissal, an' decree that 'twas all over.

Mary   Yes?

Mommo   An' 'twas.

Mary   Aa, you have more for me?

Mommo (*childlike*)   Have I?

Mary *nods.* **Mommo** *thinking her own thoughts, then she shakes her head.*

Mary   A laughing competition there would be.

Mommo (*absently*)   A what?

Dolly   She's exhausted.

Mary   She's not!

Mommo   Where was I? . . . In the jostlin' an' pushin' . . . (*Then her eyes searching the floor, in half-memory, lamenting trampled sweets.*) The sweets.

Mary   Here they are. (*The ones that* **Dolly** *brought.*)

Mommo   The sweets (*Her eyes still searching the floor.*) In the jostlin' an' pushin' . . . The sweets for her children trampled under their boots.

Dolly   Can't you see she's −

Mary   She's not.

Mommo   Phuh: dust.

Mary   But if Costello decreed 'twas all over, how did it start up again?

Mommo   How did? The small stranger, I told yeh, goin' out to check the weather for as had been forecasted the thaw was settling in.

Mary   I see!

Mommo   An' sure they could have got home.

Mary   Yes?

Mommo   They could have got home. (*Brooding, growls; then.*) Costello could decree. All others could decree. But what about the things had been vexin' *her* for years? No, a woman isn't stick or stone. The forty years an' more in the one bed together (an') he to rise in the mornin' (and) not to give her a glance. An' so long it had been he had called her by first name, she'd near forgot it herself . . . Brigit . . . Hah? . . . An' so she thought he hated her . . . An' maybe he did, like everything else . . . An'. (*Her head comes up, eyes fierce.*) 'Yis, yis-yis, he's challe'gin' ye, he is!' She gave it to the Bochtáns. And to her husband returning? – maybe he would recant, but she'd renege matters no longer. 'Och hona ho gus hah-haa!' – she hated him too.

Mary *leans back; she has not heard this part of the story before.*

Mary   . . . And what happened then?

Mommo   An' what happened then. Tried to pacify her. (*Growls.*) But there-was-none-would-assuage-her. An' what happened then, an' what happened then. 'Stand up then,' says Costello. They already standin'. 'Scath siar uaim' to the rest to clear back off the floor. The arena was ready.

Mary   And what happened then?

Mommo   An' what happened then . . . Tired, tired.

Mary   Mommo?

Mommo (*now regarding* **Mary** *with
suspicion*)   . . . . Shthap! . . . (*To herself.*) Tired . . .
What's your business here? . . . There are no newses here
for anyone about anything.

Dolly   It's ten to ten, so your father'll hardly come now,
so off with yeh to sleep. There's the good girl, and we'll
hear your confession again tomorrow night. There, there
now. (*To* **Mary**.) That was a new bit. There, there now.
She's in bye-byes.

Mary (*quietly*)   She's not.

Dolly   She's asleep! Mommo? . . . Ten to ten, 1984, and I
read it – how long ago was it? – that by 1984 we'd all be
going on our holidays to the moon in *Woman's Own*.

Mary   She's not asleep.

Dolly   I'm not arg'in' about it. She's – resting.

Mary   And I'm going to rouse her again in a minute.
You were saying?

Dolly (*stretching herself, flaunting her stomach*)   And a telly
would fit nicely over there.

Mary   A plan, a proposition, you have it all figured out?

Dolly   And I'm sorry now I spent the money on the
video. No one uses it. You'd make more use of it. It has a
remote. (*In answer to* **Mary**'s *query 'remote'.*) Yeh know? One
of them things yeh – (*hold in your hand*) –and – (*further
demonstrates*) – control.

Mary   I have a video here already (*Mommo.*) What's
your plan?

Dolly   Wait'll we have a drink. She's guilty.

Mary   Guilty of what?

Dolly   I don't know.

Mary   Then why –

Dolly I'm not arg'in' with yeh! (*Offering to top up* **Mary**'s *drink*.)

Mary Why can't you ever finish a subject or talk straight? I don't want another drink.

Dolly I'm talking straight.

Mary What's on your mind, Dolly? I'm up to you.

Dolly There's no one up to Dolly.

Mary Tck!

Dolly I'm talkin' straight!

Another car passes by outside.

Traffic. The weekend-long meeting at the computer plant place. And all the men, busy, locked outside the fence.

Mary (*abrupt movement to the table*) On second thoughts. (*And pours lemonade into her glass*.)

Dolly (*is a bit drunk and getting drunker*) No, wait a minute.

Mary What-are-you-saying, Dolly?

Dolly An' that's why she goes on like a gramophone: Guilty.

Mary This is nonsense.

Dolly And so are you.

Mary So am I!

Dolly An' you owe me a debt.

Mary What do I owe you?

Dolly *And* she *had* to get married.

Mary (*to herself*) Impossible.

Dolly No! No! – Mary? Wait a minute –

Mary (*fingers to her forehead*) Dolly, I'm –

Dolly I'm talkin' straight.

Mary   Trying to get a grip of – Ahmm. I'm trying to find
– ahmm. Get control of – ahmm. My life, Dolly.

Dolly   Yes. You're trying to say make head and tail of it
all, talk straight, like myself – No, Mary, hold on! You told
me one thing, I'll tell you another. D'yeh remember the
pony-and-trap-Sunday-outings? I don't. But I remember –
now try to contradict this – the day we buried Grandad.
Now I was his favourite so I'll never forget it. And whereas
– No, Mary! – whereas! She stood there over that hole in
the ground like a rock – like a duck, like a duck, her chest
stickin' out. Not a tear.

Mary   What good would tears have been?

Dolly   Not a tear. And – *And!* – Tom buried in that same
hole in the ground a couple of days before. Not a tear, then
or since. Oh I gathered a few 'newses' about our Mommo.

Mary   Maybe she's crying now.

Dolly   *All* of them had to get married except myself and
Old Sharp Eyes. Mrs-McGrath-the-sergeant-said. But she
bore a bastard all the same. Her Stephen. (*Wanders to the
radio and switches it off.*) The hypocrite.

Mary   Leave it on.

Dolly   I've a proposition.

Mary   It's the Sunday Concert, switch it on.

Dolly (*switches on the radio*)   So what d'yeh think?

Mary   About what?

Dolly   The slated (*Gestures roof.*), the other things I
mentioned.

Mary   It would stop the place falling down for someone
alright.

Dolly   An' half of this place is mine, I'll sign it over.

Mary   To whom?

Dolly   To *whom*. To Jack-Paddy-Andy, to Kitty-the-
Hare, to you. And there might be – other things – you
might need.

Mary   What else could anyone need?

Dolly *now looking a bit hopeless, pathetic, offering a cigarette to*
Mary, *lighting it for* **Mary**.

Dolly   An' would you like another? (*Drink*.)

Mary *shakes her head.*

Lemonade?

Mary   No. What are you trying to say?

Dolly   An' the turf out there won't last the winter.

Mary   You said that.

Dolly   And one of the children.

She looks at **Mary** *for a reaction. But all this time* **Mary**'s *mind,
or half of it, is on* **Mommo**.

Yeh. Company for yeh.

Mary   I get all this if I stay.

Dolly   Or go.

Mary (*becoming alert*)   . . . What? . . . You want me to
go? With one of the children? . . . *Which* one of the
children?

Dolly (*continues with closed eyes through the following*)   Jesus,
I'm tired. A brand new one.

Mary *laughs incredulously.*

Would you? Would you? Would you?

Mary   What?

Dolly   Take him. It.

Mary   With me?

Dolly (*nods*)   An' no one need be any the wiser.

Mary   And if I stay?

Dolly   Say it's yours. It'll all blow over in a month.

Mary   You're crazy.

Dolly   That makes three of us. I'm not crazy. I'm – as you can see.

Mary   Yes. I've wondered for some time, but I thought you couldn't – you couldn't! – be that stupid.

A car passes by outside.

Dolly   More take-aways for the lads. (*She starts wearily for her coat.*) My, but they're busy.

Mary   No one is asking you to leave.

Dolly (*stops. Eyes closed again*)   You'll be paid.

Mary   I've heard you come up with a few things before, but!

Dolly   Stephen'll kill me.

Mary   What about me?

Dolly   Or he'll cripple me.

Mary   Do you ever think of others!

Dolly   Or I'll fix him.

Mary   And you'll be out – gallivanting – again tomorrow night.

Dolly   And the night after, and the night after. And you can be sure of that.

Mary   How long are you gone?

Dolly   Five, six months.

Mary   Five, six months.

Dolly   Trying to conceal it.

Mary   Who's the father?

Dolly   I have my suspicions.

Mary   But he's busy perhaps tonight, picketing?

Dolly   Yes, very busy. Travelling at the sound of speed. But the Chinese'll get them.

Mary   And this is the help? This is what you've been figuring out?

Dolly   You can return the child after, say, a year. If you want to.

Mary   I thought your figuring things out were about – ? (*She indicates* **Mommo**. *Then she goes to* **Mommo**.) Mommo, open your eyes, time to continue.

Dolly   After a year it'll be easy to make up a story.

Mary   *Another* story! (*She laughs.*)

Dolly   You're a nurse, you could help me if you wanted to.

Mary   Trying all my life to get out of *this* situation and now you want to present me with the muddle of your stupid life to make *sure* the saga goes on.

Dolly   Oh the saga will go on.

Mary   Mommo!

Dolly   I'll see to that, one way or the other.

Mary (*to herself*)   I go away with a brand new baby. Mommo! (*To* **Dolly**.) Where! Where do I go?

Dolly *nods.*

You have that figured out too?

Dolly   We can discuss that.

Mary *laughs.*

You're its aunt.

Mary   Its! (*She laughs.*)

Dolly   Aunt! – Aunt! – Aunt!

Mary   Mommo! I know you're not asleep.

Dolly (*shrugs*)   OK. (*Now talking to herself.*) And if it's a boy you can call it Tom, and if it's a girl you can call it Tom. (*Continues through the following,* **Dolly***'s speech, though to herself, dominating.*)

Mommo   Supa milk, where's the milk?

Mary   Later. To continue. Where had you got to?

Mommo   But in the jostlin' an' pushin' (*Eyes searching the floor.*) The sweets . . . the sweets . . .

Dolly (*through the above*)   But I've discussed something with someone. 'Cause if I don't get Stephen, Stephen'll get me. But I know now how to get him and that's what got me saving, of late. I've made the preliminary enquiries. That little service of fixing someone is available – 'cause it's in demand – even round here. I've discussed the fee with someone.

Mommo   Phuh: dust.

Mary (*to* **Dolly**)   Have you finished?

Dolly (*intensely*)   You had it easy!

Mary   I had it easy? No one who came out of this – house – had it easy. (*To herself:*) I had it easy.

Dolly   You-had-it-easy. The bright one, top of your class!

Mary (*to herself*)   What would you know about it?

Dolly   Top marks! – Hardly had your Leaving Cert and you couldn't wait to be gone.

Mary   I won't deny that.

Dolly   You can't! State Registered Nurse before you were twenty –

Mary   Twenty-one –

Dolly   A Sister before you were twenty-five, Assistant Matron at the age of thirty.

Mary   And a midwife.

Dolly   Yes, SRN, CMB, DDT!

Mary   All very easy.

Dolly   Couldn't get away fast enough.

Mary   But I came back, Dolly.

Dolly   Aren't you great?

Mary   I failed. It all failed. I'm as big a failure as you, and that's some failure.

Dolly *is stopped for a moment by* **Mary**'s *admission.*

You hadn't considered that?

Mommo *has started rambling again, repeating the last section of the story which she told earlier, down to 'The arena was ready'.*

Mommo   An' sure they could have got home. They could have got home. Costello could decree . . .

Dolly (*her voice over* **Mommo**'s)   No! No! You had it easy! – You had it – You had – I had – I had ten! – I had a lifetime! – A lifetime! – Here with herself, doin' her every bidding, listenin' to her seafóid (*rambling*) gettin' worse till I didn't know where I was! – Pissin' in the bed beside me – I had a lifetime! Then the great Stephen – the surprise of it! comes coortin'! Never once felt any – real – warmth from him – what's wrong with him? – but he's my rescuer, my saviour. But then, no rhyme or reason to it – He could've got a job at that plant, but he couldn't wait to be gone either! Then waitin' for the hero, my rescuer, the sun shining out of his eighty-five-pounds-a-week arse, to come home at Christmas. No interest in me – oh, he used me! – or in children, or the rotten thatch or the broken window, or Conor above moving in his fence from *this* side. I'm

fightin' all the battles. Still fightin' the battles. And what
d'yeh think he's doin' now this minute? Sittin' by the
hearth in Coventry, is he? Last Christmas an' he was
hardly off the bus, Old Sharp Eyes whisperin' into his ear
about me. Oooo, but he waited. Jesus, how I hate him!
Jesus, how I hate them! Men! Had his fun and games with
me that night, *and* first thing in the morning. Even sat
down to eat the hearty breakfast I made. Me thinkin', still
no warmth, but maybe it's goin' to be okay. Oooo, but I
should've known from *experience* about-the-great-up-stand-
in'-Steph-en-evrabody's-fav-our-ite. Because, next thing he
has me by the hair of the head, fistin' me down in the
mouth. Old Sharp Eyes there, noddin' her head every time
he struck an' struck an' kicked an' kicked an' pulled me
round the house by the hair of the head. Jesus, men!
(*Indicating the outdoors where she had her sex.*) You-think-I-
enjoy? I-use-*them*! Jesus, hypocrisy! An' then, me left with
my face like a balloon – you saw a lot of me last Christmas'
didn't yeh? – my body black and blue, the street angel an'
his religious mother – 'As true as Our Lady is in heaven
now, darlin's' – over the road to visit you an' Mommo
with a little present an' a happy an' a holy Christmas now
darlin's an' blessed St-fuckin'-Jude an' all the rest of them
flyin' about for themselves up there.

Mommo   The arena was ready. A laughing competition
there would be. (*She coughs in preparation.*) 'Wuff-a-wuff.'

Dolly   Jesus, how I hate them! I hate her (*Mommo*) – I
hate this house – She hates you – I hate my own new
liquorice-all-sorts-coloured house –

Mary, **Dolly** *speaking simultaneously.*

Mary (*ashen-face, shaking her head*)   No . . . No.

Dolly   She! – She! – She hates you!

Mary   No.

Mommo, **Dolly** *speaking simultaneously.*

Mommo 'Wuff a wuff! A wuha wuha wuha wuha –
Naaw.'

Dolly And I hate you!

Mary Why?

Dolly Why! You don't know terror, you don't know
hatred, you don't know desperation!

Mommo An' sure Costello's laughin' wasn't right at all.

Dolly No one came out of this house had it easy but you
had it easy.

Mommo *unwraps a sweet and sucks it.*

Mary Dolly, stop it at once!

Dolly 'Dolly, stop it at once.' Look, go away an' stay
away.

Mary Dolly!

Dolly 'This is our home' – You'll need a few bob. I'll
give it to you, and my grand plan: I'll look after things
here, all fronts, including lovee lovee Mommo, an'
Stephen'll never raise a finger to me again.

Mary You're –

Dolly Am I?

Mary You're –

Dolly Am I? We'll see – Hah! – if I'm bluffing.

Mary Have you finished ranting?

Dolly Ooh, 'ranting!'

Mary You're spoilt, you're unhappy, you're running
round in circles.

Dolly *I'm* running round in circles? Suitcase packed –
How many times? Puttin' on airs – look at the boots, look
at the lady! You're stayin', you're goin', 'I need to talk to

someone' – Fuck off! 'I wanted to come home, I had to come home' – Fuck off!

Mary   Stop it this moment, I won't have it! You're frightening her.

In reply to 'frightening her', **Dolly** *indicates* **Mommo** *who is sucking a sweet, lost in her own thoughts. Then* **Dolly** *turns her back to* **Mary***; she continues in quieter tone.*

Dolly   The countryside produced a few sensations in the last couple of years, but my grand plan: I'll show them what can happen at the dark of night in a field. I'll come to grips with my life.

Short silence.

Mommo*'s eyes fixed on* **Mary***.*

Mommo   Miss? . . . Do I know you?

Mary *shakes her head, 'No'; she is afraid to speak; if she does she will cry.*

. . . Pardon?

Mary *shakes her head.*

Dolly (*to the fire*)   I'll finish another part of this family's history in grander style than any of the others.

Mary   . . . The arena was ready.

Mommo   'Twas.

Mary   But Costello's laugh wasn't right at all.

Mommo   Then ''Scuse me a minute,' says he lickin' his big mouth, puts a spit in the one hand, then one in the other, an' ponders the third that he sent to the floor. (*Coughs.*) 'A wuff.'

Dolly   A wuff, wuff!

Mommo   'A wuha wuha wuha wuha, a wuha huha huha hoo, quawk awk-awk-awk a ho ho ho, a wo ho ho ho ho ho ho!' An' twasn't bad at all. Was it? An' Costello knew it.

An' by way of exper'ment, though 'twasn't his turn, had a go at it again, his ear cocked to himself.

Dolly We filled half that graveyard. Well, I'll fill the other half.

Mommo Then, ''Scuse me too,' says the stranger makin' Costello, stiffen, an' 'Heh heh heh, heh heh heh, heh heh heh,' chuckled he.

Dolly Heh heh heh, heh heh heh, heh heh heh –

Mary (*ferociously at* **Dolly**) Shthap!

Mommo . . . Miss?

Mary (*to* **Mommo**) . . . No, you don't know me. But I was here once, and I ran away to try and blot out here. I didn't have it easy. Then I tried bad things, for a time, with someone. So then I came back, thinking I'd find – something – here, or, if I didn't, I'd put everything right. And tonight I thought I'd make a last try. Mommo? Live out the – story – finish it, move on to a place where, perhaps, we could make some kind of new start. Mommo?

Mommo Where's the milk for the night?

Mary *nods that she will get it.*

Mommo Tck!

Mary (*gently to* **Dolly**) She may hate me, you may hate me. But I don't hate her. I love her for what she's been through, and she's all that I have. So she has to be my only consideration. She doesn't understand. Do you understand, Dolly? Please . . . And I'm sorry.

Dolly (*drunkenly*) For what?

Mary (*turns away tearfully*) I'm not the saint you think I am.

Dolly The what? Saint? That'd be an awful thing to be. 'Wo ho ho, ho ho ho!'

Mary *puts the milk by the bed.*

Mommo   Yis. Did ye hear? The full style *was* returnin' –
'Wo ho ho, wo ho ho!' An' like a great archbishop turnin'
on his axis, nods an' winks to his minions that he knew all
along. The cheers that went up in John Mah'ny's that
night!

Now what did they start doin', the two gladiators,
circlin' the floor, eyes riveted together, silent in quietude to
find the advantage, save the odd whoop from Costello, his
fist through the ceilin', an' the small little stranger'd bate
the odd little dance.

Now. Then. And.

'Yeh sold all your cargo?' Costello roarin' like a master
to friken a scholar. The laugh from his attendants, but
then so did the stranger.

'Where (*are*) yeh bound for?' – stern Costello – 'Your
destination, a Mhico?'

'Ballindineside, your worship.'

'Ballindineside, a Thighearna!'

Dolly   Oh ho ho, wo ho ho.

Mommo   'Cunn ether iss syha soory.' (*Coinn iotair is
saidhthe suaraighe*)

Dolly   Hounds of rage and bitches of wickedness!

Mommo   An' the description despicable more fitting
their own place.

Dolly (*to the fire, almost dreamily*)   Why the fuck did he
marry me?

Mommo   'A farmer?' says Costello. 'A goose one,' says
the stranger. An' t'be fair to the Bochtáns they plauded the
self-denigration.

Dolly   I don't hate anyone.

Mommo   'An' yourself?' says the stranger. 'Oh now
you're questionin' me,' says Costello, 'An' Rabbits,'
screeches Josie, 'Hull-hull-hull, hull-hull-hull!'

Dolly (*stands*)   What did I get up for?

Mary *and* **Dolly** *forget themselves and start laughing at* **Mommo**'s *dramatisation of this section.*

Mommo   An' Rabbits!' says the stranger. 'Rabbits!' saying he. 'Well, heh heh heh, heh heh heh, heh heh heh, heh heh heh!' 'What's the cause of your laughter?' Costello frownin' moroya. (*Mar dhea; pretending seriousness*) 'Bunny rabbits! says the stranger – is *that* what you're in!'

'Not at all, me little man,' says Costello, 'I've a herd of trinamanooses in Closh back the road.'
   'Tame ones?' says the stranger.
   'Tame ones, what else, of a certainty,' says Costello, 'An' the finest breed for 'atin' sure!'
   'But for the Townies though for 'atin',' says the stranger, most sincerely. An' not able to keep the straight face, Costello roared out a laughter, an' gave beck to his attendants to plaud the stranger's cleverality.

Now wasn't he able for them?

Dolly   Where's the flashlamp?

Mommo   An' the contrariety an' venom was in it while ago!

Dolly   I want to go out the back.

Mary   It's on top of the dresser.

Mommo   (But now they couldn't do enough for that decent man an' woman, all vying with each other – an' sure they didn't have it – to buy treats for the strangers, tumblers of whiskey an' bumpers of port wine.) A strange auld world right enough. But in some wisdom of his own He made it this way. 'Twas like the nicest night ever.

Dolly (*has got the flashlamp; a plea in her voice*)   Mary?

Mary   'Twas like the nicest night ever.

Mommo   But they'd yet to find the topic would keep them laughin' near forever.

Dolly   Mary?

Mary   Topic?

Mommo   Then one'd laugh solo, the other'd return it, then Costello'd go winkin' an' they'd both laugh together, a nod from the stranger (*and*) they'd stop that same moment to urge riotous chorus, give the others a chance.

Dolly   Don't want the fuggin' flashlamp. (*She discards it. Then, as if driving cattle out of the house, she goes out the back door.*) How! – How! – How! Hup! – Skelong! – Bleddy cows! Howa-that-how! – Hup! Hup! . . .

Mary   What topic did they find?

Mommo   But there can be no gainsayin' it, Costello clear had the quality laugh. 'Wo ho ho, ho ho ho': (in) the barrel of his chest would great rumbles start risin', rich rolls of round sound out of his mouth, to explode in the air an' echo back rev'berations. An' next time demonstratin' the range of his skill, go flyin' aloft (to) the heights of registration – 'Hickle-ickle-ickle-ickle!' – like a hen runnin' demented from the ardent attentions of a cock in the yard after his business. Now!

Mary   What about Grandad?

Mommo   Who?

Mary   The stranger.

Mommo   Not much by way of big sound?

Mary   No.

Mommo   Or rebounding modulation?

Mary   No.

Mommo   But was that a stipulation?

Mary   No.

Mommo   He knew the tricks of providence and was cunning of exertion. Scorn for his style betimes?

Mary *nods.*

But them wor his tactics.

Mary   And he was the one most in control.

Mommo   He was. (*She yawns.*) Tired.

Mary   ˙No, Mommo. It *is* a nice story. And you've nearly told it all tonight. Except for the last piece that you never tell.

Mommo   Who was that woman?

Mary   What woman?

Mommo   Tck! – The woman just went out the door there. (*Mimicking* **Dolly**.) 'Hup-hup-howa that'!

Mary   That was Dolly . . . Dolly.

Mommo   An' does she always behave that way?

Mary   Sometimes.

Mommo (*thinking about this; it does not make sense to her. Then eyes scrutinising* **Mary**: *in this moment she is possibly close to recognising* **Mary**)   . . . Who are (*you*)?

Mary   Try a guess. Yes, Mommo? – Yes, Mommo? – Please – who am I?

Mommo   Here she is again!

Dolly *comes in. She looks bloated and tired. She wolfs down the slice of cake which she deliberately resisted earlier. Then looking for her bag, putting on her overcoat, etc.*

Dolly   And I've been starving myself.

Mommo (*whispering*)   She'd eat yeh out of house an' home . . . Is there something you require, Miss, that you're rummaging for over there?

Dolly (*realises she is being spoken to*)   Your pension.

Mommo   Oh it's time for ye both to be going – ten to ten. He doesn't like calling when there's strangers in the house.

Mary   We're off now in a minute. What was that topic again that kept them on laughing?

Mommo   Misfortunes. (*She yawns*.)

Mary   Mommo? (**Mommo**'s *eyes are closed*.)

Dolly (*to herself, looking at the door*)   I hate going home.

Mary   Or if you like, the bit about 'Out of the bushes more of them were comin'.'

Mommo   Tom is in Galway. (*Opens her eyes*.) I bet him with nettles. Mitchin' from school. D'yeh think he remembers?

Mary (*gently*)   No.

Mommo (*closes her eyes*)   Well, I don't remember . . . I don't remember any more of it.

Mary (*tired, futile*)   And out of the bushes more of them were coming, wherever their hovels were, holes in the ground . . . 'cause 'twas place of desolation.

Dolly   . . . What were you trying to do with her?

Mary   'Twas only a notion . . . She's asleep.

Dolly   Maybe she'd wake up again?

Mary (*slight shake of her head, 'No'*)   Sit down.

Dolly   What're yeh goin' to do?

Mary (*slight shake of her head, a tremulous sigh*)   Ahmm.

Dolly   Back to the nursing?

Mary   No. That wasn't me at all. And no confidence now anyway. (*She collects up a few odds and ends and puts them in the suitcase*.) Who's looking after the children?

Dolly   Maisie Kelly. They're stayin' the night in her house.

Mary (*absently*)   The nicest night ever.

Dolly   . . . What were we doin' that night?

Mary   Ahmm. The shade on that light: do you mind if I? (*She switches off the light and lights a candle.*) We let the fire go out. The cursèd paraffin. (*She switches off the radio?*)

Mary *has collected up a silver-backed hairbrush and a clothes brush.*

Dolly   . . . But if you're not going back to the nursing?

Mary   There must be *some* future for me, somewhere. (*She is brushing the back of* **Dolly**'*s coat*.) I can certainly scrub floors.

Dolly (*a little irritably*)   What're you doin'?

Mary   Just a little – dust – here.

Dolly   Who cares?

Mary   It's just that people talk at the slightest.

Dolly   Do you care what people say?

Mary   I'm afraid I do. There. (*Coat brushed; she now brushes* **Dolly**'*s hair*.) When I was a nurse there was a patient, terminal, an elderly woman and we became very close. I don't know why she used to watch me or why she chose to make friends with me.

Dolly   What are you doin' now?

Mary   But one day she said, in the middle of – whatever – conversation we were having. 'You're going to be alright, Mary.' Simple remark. But it took me by surprise. It was like, a *promised* blessing. And why I should have – (*Shrugs.*) believed in it for, oh, twenty years? until recently, I don't know. There. (**Dolly**'*s hair is brushed*.) She left me these (*The brushes.*) and this (*The teapot.*) and the book. (*She dumps the lot into the suitcase.*)

Dolly   If I sat down to write a book.

Mary   Though the book has always depressed me a bit. *Winter Words*. I can't do a thing for you, Dolly. Can you lend me a hundred quid?

Dolly *nods*.

Well, that's it then.

Dolly *is just sitting there looking into the fire;* **Mary** *standing: two figures frozen in time. Then the cortège of cars approaching, passing the house (at comparatively slow speed).*

Dolly   The funeral. The weekend-long meeting is over. Now are they travelling at the sound of speed?

Mary *laughs*.

I told you the Chinese'd get them.

(*They are beginning to laugh. Looking at her stomach – the bulge.*) Good man Josie!

Mary *laughs*. **Dolly** *joins in the laughter,* **Dolly** *flaunting herself, clowning.*

And you're 'Josie's' aunt!

They laugh louder, the laughter getting out of hand.

(*To her stomach.*)   Good man Josie! . . . (*Uproariously.*) Jesus, misfortunes!

Then the unexpected, **Mommo**'s *voice.*

Mommo   What time is it?

Silence.

Mary   Seven. (*In a whisper, waiting, frozen.*)

Mommo   Explosions of laughter an' shouts of hurrahs!

Dolly (*sits heavily on the bed*)   Jesus, I'm tired.

Mary (*pleading with* **Dolly**)   Dolly!

Mommo   For excess of joy.

Dolly   'S alright, 'salright, Mommo: I'm Dolly, I'm like a film star. (*She lies back on the bed.*)

Mommo   An' didn't he ferret out her eyes to see how she was farin', an' wasn't she titherin' with the best of them an' weltin' her thighs. No heed on her now to be gettin' on home. No. But offerin' to herself her own congratulations at hearin' herself laughin'. An' then, like a girl, smiled at her husband, an' his smile back so shy, like the boy he was in youth. An' the moment was for them alone. Unaware of all cares, unaware of all the others. An' how long before since their eyes had met, mar gheal dhá gréine, glowing love for each other. Not since long and long ago.

And now Costello's big hand was up for to call a recession. 'But how,' says he, 'is it to be indisputably decided who is the winner?' And a great silence followed. None was forgettin' this was a contest. An' the eyes that wor dancin', now pending the answer, glazed an' grave in dilation: 'Twas a difficult question. (*Quietly.*) Och-caw. Tired of waiting male intelligence, 'He who laughs last', says she.

An' 'cause 'twas a woman that spoke it, I think Costello was frikened, darts class of a glance at her an' – (*She gulps.*) 'That's what I thought,' says he.

But wasn't that his mistake? ever callin' the recession an' he in full flight. 'Cause now, ready himself as he would, with his coughin' an' spittin', the sound emanating from a man of his talent, so forced and ungracious, he'd stop it himself.

(*Whispering.*) 'He's lost it,' says someone (Her derisory shout on the night.) Och hona ho gus hah-haa!
(*Whispering.*) 'He should never have stopped.' Their faces like mice.

An' he'd 'tempt it an' 'tempt it an' 'tempt it again. Ach an fear mór as Bochtán (*But the big man from Bochtán*) in respiratory disaster is i ngreas casachtaí (*and in bouts of coughing*)   (*She coughs . . .*) The contest was over.

Mary   The contest was over?

Mommo   'Twas.

Mary   The contest was over?

Mommo   Oh the strangers'd won.

Mary   But what about the topic?

Mommo   Hah?

Mary   Would keep them laughing near forever.

Mommo (*whispers*)   Misfortunes . . . *She* supplied them
with the topic. And it started up again with the subject of
potatoes, the damnedable crop was in that year.
   'Wet an' wat'rey?' says the stranger.
   'Wet an' wat'rey,' laughing Costello.
   'Heh heh heh, but not blighted?'
   'No ho ho, ho ho ho, but scabby an' small.'
   'Sour an' soapy – Heh heh heh.'
   'Yis – ho ho,' says the hero. 'Hard to wash, ladies, hard
to boil, ladies?'
   'An' the divil t'ate – Heh heh heh!'
But they were only getting into their stride.
   'An' the hay?' says old Brian, 'behell.'
   'Rotted!' says the contestants, roarin' it together.
   'The bita oats,' shouts young Kemple – 'Jasus!' Lodged
in the field. An' the turf says another. Still in the bog,
laughed the answer, an' the chickens the pip, pipes up the
old crone. An' the sheep, the staggers, an' the cow that just
died, an' the man that was in it lost both arms to the
thresher, an' the *dead!*

Mary   . . . And the dead, Mommo? Who were the dead?

Mommo   Skitherin' an' laughin' – Hih-hih-hih – at their
nearest an' dearest. Her Pat was her eldest, died of
consumption, had his pick of the girls an' married the
widdy again' all her wishes. The decline in that fambly,
she knew the widdy'd outlast him. She told them the story
– Hih-hih-hih – an' many another. An' how Pat, had come
back for the two sheep (*that*) wor his – An' they wor – An'
he was her first-born. But you'll not have them she told

him. Shy Willie inside, quiet by the hearth, but she knew
he'd be able, the spawgs of hands he had on him. 'Is it
goin' fightin' me own brother?' But she told him a brother
was one thing, but she was his mother, an' them were her
orders to give Pat the high road, and no sheep, one, two or
three wor leavin' the yard. They hurted each other. An'
how Pat went back empty to his strap of a widdy, an' was
dead within a six months. Hih-hih-hih. (*The 'hih-hih-hih'
which punctuate her story sound more like ingrown sobs rather than
laughter*.) Oh she made great contributions, rollcalling the
dead. Was she what or 'toxicated? An' for the sake of an
auld ewe stuck in the flood was how she lost two of the
others, Jimmy and Michael. Great gales of laughter
following each name of the departed. Hih-hih-hih. An' the
nice wife was near her time, which one of them left behind
him?

Mary   Daddy.

Mommo   Died tryin' to give birth to the fourth was to be
in it. An' she herself left with the care of three small childre
waitin'. All contributions receiving volleys of cheers.
Nothin' was sacred an' nothing a secret. The unbaptised
an' stillborn in shoeboxes planted, at the dead hour of
night treading softly the Lisheen to make the regulation
hole. Not more, not less than two feet deep. And too fearful
of the field, haunted by infants, to speak or to pray. They
were fearful for their ankles – Hih-hih-hih. An' tryin' not
to hasten, steal away again, leaving their pagan parcels in
isolation forever. Hih-hih-hih. And Willie too, her pet,
went foreign after the others. An' *did* she drive them all
away? Never ever to be heard of, ever again: Save shy
Willie, aged thirty-four, in Louisaville Kentucky, died,
peritonites. Spell that. A-N-T Yes? I-P-H. Yes? F-U-L-
Yes? L-O-G- Yes? E-S-T- Yes? I-N-E- Antiphfullogestine,
Now! That's how I taught them all to spell. Hih-hih-hih!
The nicest night they ever had, that's what I'm sayin'. She
kept the stories comin'. And all of them present, their
heads threwn back abandoned in festivities of guffaws: the
wretched and neglected, dilapidated an' forlorn, the

forgotten an' tormented, the lonely an' despairing, ragged an' dirty, impoverished, hungry, emaciated and unhealthy, eyes big as saucers, ridiculing an' defying of their lot on earth below – glintin' their defiance – their defiance an' rejection, inviting of what else might come or *care* to come! – driving bellows of refusal at the sky through the roof. Och hona ho gus hah-haa!

Mary   An' what else was to come?

Mommo   Nothing.

Mary   Tom.

Mommo   Tom is in Galway.

Mary   Grandad.

Mommo   An' when I told me father what did he say? ''Twas an insolence at heaven.' Sure we weren't meant to be here at all! 'Making mock of God's prize piece, its structure and system.' 'Oh,' he groaned. 'I have wrestled with enigmals (*all*) my life-long years, I've combed all of creation,' that man intoned, 'and in the wondrous handiwork of God, have found only two flaws, man an' the earwig. Of what use is man, what utility the earwig, where do they either fit in the system? They are both specimens desperate, without any control, and therefore unfree. One cocks his head,' says he, 'the other his tail. But God will not be mocked. Especially when He was so clever at creating all things else. Still, God must have said, I'll leave them there an' see what transpires.' An' says me father – (*She winks shrewdly.*) 'Maybe the earwig isn't doin' too bad at all.' . . . 'Twas an insolence at heaven. But they'd soon get their answer.

Mary   Who would?

Mommo   The Bochtáns, the Bochtáns sure! Tck! Mauleogs drunk?

Mary *nods.*

Them all packed together?

Mary *nods.*

The foul odour that was in it, you'd hardly get your breath. The two contestants sweating, the big man most profusely – Sure they'd been contending the title now five or six hours. An' Costello, openin' down his shirts an' loosenin' his buckle, was doublin' up an' staggerin' an' holdin' his sides. 'Aw Jasus, lads, ye have me killed – Hickle-ickle-ickle,' an' the laughing lines upon his mien wor more like lines of pain. An' the stranger 'Heh heh heh heh, heh heh heh heh,' aisy an' gentle. Then beholding his 'ponent from contortion to convulsion, his complexion changin' colours an' arrivin' at purple: 'Heh heh heh heh, heh heh . . . heh . . . heh,' the frown to his brow bringin' stillness upon him an' the two little smiles to the sides of his mouth. Suddenly he shouts, 'Costello's the winner!' But sure they wouldn't have it – nor herself in the corner. 'He's nat (*not*), he's nat, he's nat, he's nat!' 'On, on-on, Bochtán forever!'

'No-no! – Heh-heh – he has me bet!'

'He's nat, he's nat, he's nat, he's nat!'

The others, 'Up Bochtán! Bochtán forever!'

An' Costello now all the while in upper registration – 'Hickle-ickle-ickle-ickle' – longin' to put stop to it, his own cacklin' wouldn't let him. An' 'deed, when he'd 'tempt to rise an arm – an' sure he wasn't able – in gesture of cessation, th' others mistakin' of his purpose would go thinkin' t' do it for'm (*for him*) puncturin' holes in the ceilin', batin' stomps on the floor.

An' the stranger now could only stand and watch. An' late it was herself realised the Great Adversary had entered.

'Hickle-ickle-ickle-ickle – Aw Jasus, lads, I'm dyin' – Oh not without effort. Hickle, ickle, ickle, ickle. Then slow in a swoon he went down to the floor. For the last moments were left him 'twas the stranger that held him, for there was nothing now in the world to save him, or able to save him.

Mary   And what's the rest of it? Only a little bit left.

Mommo (*musing*)   For there was nothing now in the world to save him . . .

Dolly   Mary? (*Opening her eyes for a moment.*)

Mary (*regards her gravely; then*)   You're going to be alright, Dolly. Roll in under the blanket.

Dolly *goes back to sleep.*

Mommo   Or able to save him. Did I not say that? Oh yis. 'An' the rabbits, lads,' says Cost'llo, 'I didn't sell e'er the one of them, but threwn them comin' home for fun again' Patch Curran's door.' And that was the last he was to utter that night or any other.

Mary   They don't laugh there anymore.

Mommo   Save the childre, until they arrive at the age of reason. Now! Bochtán forever is Bailegangaire.

Through the following **Mary** *undresses behind the headboard and puts on her long simple nightdress; she lets down her hair, gets the hairbrush from the case and brushes her hair. Switches off the radio. She looks remarkably beautiful; she is like a young elegant woman, her face introspective and grave.*

Mary   To conclude.

Mommo   To conclude. The thaw as was forecasted was in it, an' the strangers went home.

Mary   But didn't they hurt grandad? The stranger, his ribs?

Mommo   But he bet them – he bet the best of them.

Mary   And wasn't his face cut?

Mommo   'Twas. They wor for lettin' them home, d'yeh know? Home without hinder. Till the thief, Josie, started cryin' at death, and was demanding the boots be took of the stranger to affirm 'twas feet or no was in them. An' from trying to quieten his excitation someone of them got hit. Then he struck back. Till they forgot what they wor doin' sure, or how it had started, but all drawin' kicks an' blows,

one upon the other, till the venom went rampant. They
pulled him down off the cart an' gave him the kickin'. Oh
they gave him such a doin', till John Mah'ny an' the curate
(*that*) was called prevailed again' the Bolsheviks.

'Twas dawn when they got home. Not without
trepidation? But the three small childre, like ye, their care,
wor safe an' sound fast asleep on the settle. Now, my
fondlings, settle down an' be sayin' yere prayers. I forget
what happened the three sticks of rock. Hail Holy Queen.
Yes? Mother of Mercy. Yes? Hail our lives? Yes? Our
sweetness and our hope.

Mary   It was a bad year for the crops, a good one for
mushrooms, and the three small children were waiting for
their gran and their grandad to come home. Mommo? My
bit. Mary was the eldest. She was the clever one, and she
was seven. Dolly, the second, was like a film-star and she
was grandad's favourite. And they were in and out of the
road watching for the horse and cart. Waiting for ribbons.
And Tom who was the youngest, when he got excited
would go pacing o'er and o'er the boundary of the yard.
He had confided in Mary his expectation. They would be
bringing him his dearest wish – grandad told him secretly
– a mouth organ for Christmas. That was alright. But in
the – excitation – of their waiting they forgot to pay
attention to the fire. Then Mary and Dolly heard – 'twas
like an explosion. Tom had got the paraffin and, not the
careful way grandad did it, shhtiolled it on to the embers,
and the sudden blaze came out on top of him. And when
they ran in and . . . saw him, Mary got . . . hysterical.
Then Mary sent Dolly across the fields for May Glynn.
And sure May was only . . . eleven? Then Mary
covered . . . the wounds . . . from the bag of flour in the
corner. She'd be better now, and quicker now, at knowing
what to do. And then May Glynn's mother came and they
took Tom away to Galway, where he died . . . Two
mornings later, and he had only just put the kettle on the
hook, didn't grandad, the stranger, go down too, slow in a
swoon . . . Mommo?

Mommo   It got him at last.

Mary   Will you take your pills now?

Mommo   The yellow ones.

Mary   Yes.

Mommo   Poor Séamus.

Mommo *takes the pills with a sup of milk.*

Mary   Is there anything else you need?

Mommo   To thee do we cry. Yes? Poor banished children of Eve.

Mary   Is there anything you have to say to me?

Mommo   Be sayin' yere prayers now an' ye'll be goin' to sleep. To thee do we send up our sighs. Yes? For yere Mammy an' Daddy an' grandad is (*who are*) in heaven.

Mary   And Tom.

Mommo   Yes. An' he only a ladeen was afeared of the gander. An' tell them ye're all good. Mourning and weeping in this valley of tears. (*She is handing the cup back to* **Mary**.) And sure a tear isn't such a bad thing, Mary, and haven't we everything we need here, the two of us. (*And she settles down to sleep.*)

Mary (*tears of gratitude brim to her eyes*)   Oh we have, Mommo.

She gets into the bed with **Mommo** *and* **Dolly**. *Her tears continue to the end but she is smiling a gentle smile.*

. . . To conclude. It's a strange old place alright, in whatever wisdom He has to have made it this way. But in whatever wisdom there is, in the year 1984, it was decided to give that – fambly . . . of strangers another chance, and a brand new baby to gladden their home.

Schubert's 'Notturno' *comes in under* **Mary**'*s final speech.*

Printed in the United Kingdom
by Lightning Source UK Ltd.
103924UKS00001B/12